MW01698005

WORLD TALES

The extraordinary coincidence of stories told in all times, in all places

Copyright © The Estate of Idries Shah

The right of the Estate of Idries Shah to be identified as the owner of this work has been asserted by it in accordance with the Copyright, Designs and Patents Act 1988.

All rights reserved
Copyright throughout the world

ISBN 978-1-78479-228-2

First published 1979
Published in this edition 2015

No part of this publication may be reproduced or transmitted in any form or by any means, electronic, mechanical or photographic, by recording or any information storage or retrieval system or method now known or to be invented or adapted, without prior permission obtained in writing from the publisher, ISF Publishing, except by a reviewer quoting brief passages in a review written for inclusion in a journal, magazine, newspaper, blog or broadcast.

Requests for permission to reprint, reproduce etc., to:
The Permissions Department
ISF Publishing
The Idries Shah Foundation
P. O. Box 71911
London NW2 9QA
United Kingdom
permissions@isf-publishing.org

In association with The Idries Shah Foundation

The ISF Collectors' Library

Tales of A Parrot and Other Stories

The Happiest Man in The World
and Other Stories

The Food of Paradise
and Other Stories

The Water of Life and Other Stories

The Land Where Time Stood Still
and Other Stories

This special edition of *World Tales*
is limited to five hundred copies.

Of which this is number 196.

Tales of A Parrot and Other Stories

VOLUME I

Collected by
IDRIES SHAH

The ISF Collectors' Library

'That lurking air of hidden meanings and immemorial mythical signs which we find in some fables, recalling a people, wise and childish at once, who had built up a theory of the world ages before Aesop was born.'
— Ernest Rhys, 1925

'The content of folklore is metaphysics. Our inability to see this is due primarily to our abysmal ignorance of metaphysics and its technical terms.'
— A. K. Coomaraswamy

'The folktale is the primer of the picture-language of the soul.'
—Joseph Campbell

'They (tales) appeal to our rational and irrational instincts, to our visions and dreams… The race is richer in human and cultural values for its splendid heritage of old magic tales.'
— Dr Leonard W. Roberts

Introduction

It is quite usual to find collections of tales arranged according to language or country: *Tales of Belgium*, *Stories from the German*, or *Legends from the Indian Peoples*; some such titles must have met your eye at one time or another. It all looks very tidy, scientific even; and the study of stories is indeed a part of scholarly research.

But the deeper you go into things, the more mysterious, exciting, baffling they become. How can it be that the same story is found in Scotland and also in pre-Columbian America? Was the story of Aladdin and his Wonderful Lamp really taken from Wales (where it has been found) to the ancient East; and, if so, by whom and when? A classical Japanese narrative is part of the gypsy repertoire in Europe; where shall we pigeonhole it in national terms?

I have selected and place before you a collection of tales of which one at least goes back to the ancient Egyptian of several thousand years ago. It is presented here not to impress the reader with its age, but because it is entertaining, and also because, although the Pharaohs died out many centuries ago, this tale is recited by people all over the world who know nothing of its origins. This form of culture remains when nations, languages and faiths have long since died.

There is an almost uncanny persistence and

durability in the tale which cannot be accounted for in the present state of knowledge. Not only does it constantly appear in different incarnations which can be mapped – as the Tar-Baby story carried from Africa to America, and medieval Arabian stories from the Saracens in Sicily to the Italy of today – but from time to time remarkable collections are assembled and enjoy a phenomenal vogue: after which they lapse and are reborn, perhaps in another culture, perhaps centuries later: to delight, attract, thrill, captivate yet another audience.

Such was the great *Panchatantra*, the Far Eastern collection of tales for the education of Indian princes; the Jataka Buddhist birth-stories believed to date back two and a half thousand years; the *Thousand and One Nights*, known as 'The Mother of Tales'. Later came the collections of Straparola, Boccaccio, Chaucer and Shakespeare, and a dozen others which now form the very basis of the classical literature of Europe and Asia.

This book contains stories from all of these collections, and many more: because there is a certain basic fund of human fictions which recur, again and again, and never seem to lose their compelling attraction. Many traditional tales have a surface meaning (perhaps just a socially uplifting one) and a secondary, inner significance, which is rarely glimpsed consciously, but which nevertheless acts powerfully upon our minds. Tales have always been used, so far as we can judge, for spiritual as well as social purposes: and as parables with more or less obvious meanings this use is familiar to most people today. But, as Professor Geoffrey Parrinder says of the myth, 'its inner truth was realised when the participant was transported into the realm of the sacred and eternal.'*

Perhaps above all the tale fulfils the function not of escape but of hope. The suspending of ordinary constraints helps people to reclaim optimism and to fuel the imagination with energy for the attainment of goals: whether moral or material. Maxim Gorky realised this when he wrote: 'In tales people fly through the air on a magic carpet, walk in seven-league boots, build castles overnight; the tales opened up for me a new world where some free and all-fearless power reigned and inspired in me a dream of a better life.'

When relatively recent collectors of tales, such as Hans Christian Andersen, the Brothers Grimm, Perrault and others made their selections, they both re-established certain powerful tales in our cultures and left out others from the very vast riches of the world reservoir of stories. Paradoxically, by their very success in imprinting Cinderella, Puss-in-Boots and Beauty and the Beast anew for the modern reader (they are all very ancient tales, widely dispersed) they directed attention away from some of the most wonderful and arresting stories which did not feature

* G. Parrinder, Foreword to *Pears Encyclopaedia of Myths and Legends*, London 1976, p.10.

in their collections. Many of these stories are represented here.

Working for thirty-five years among the written and oral sources of our world heritage in tales, one feels a truly living element in them which is startlingly evident when one isolates the 'basic' stories: the ones which tend to have travelled farthest, to have featured in the largest number of classical collections, to have inspired great writers of the past and present.

One becomes aware, by this contact with the fund of tradition which constantly cries out to be projected anew, that the story in some elusive way is the basic form and inspiration. Thought or style, characterisation and belief, didactic and nationality, all recede to give place to the tale which feels almost as if it is demanding to be reborn through one's efforts. And yet those efforts themselves, in some strange way, are experienced as no more than the relatively poor expertise of the humblest midwife. It is the tale itself, when it emerges, which is king.

Erskine Caldwell, no less, has felt a similar power in the story, and is well aware of its primacy over mere thought of philosophy: 'A writer,' he says (*Atlantic Monthly*, July 1958) 'is not a great mind, he's not a great thinker, he's not a great philosopher, he's a story-teller.'

Idries Shah

Note: This is the full introduction as it appeared in the original version of *World Tales*

Contents

Tales of a Parrot

An ancient Sanskrit work, now lost, is believed to be the original of the Parrot Tales, which have been found in folk-recitals from Indonesia to Italy. The 14th century Persian Tuti Nama *(Parrot Book) by Nakhshabi is the collection of linked tales best known in the East, and it is still very widely read and recited. There is a derivative Sanskrit version, the* Seventy Parrot Tales. *Many of these stories, told by a parrot to divert his mistress while her husband is away, are found in the medieval* Seven Wise Masters, *which circulated for centuries in Europe with a popularity second only to the Bible. The book is found in Greek, Hebrew, and other languages. The first European version is thought to have been prepared by the monk Johannes, of the French diocese of Nancy, in about 1184 AD. The tales are thought to have been dispersed among the people of the West by wandering preachers. 'By such means,' says the eminent scholar Clouston, 'stories, which had their birth in the Far East more*

than two thousand years ago, spread into the remotest nooks of Europe; and jests, which had long shaken the shoulders and wagged the beards of grave and otiose Orientals, became naturalised from cold Sweden to sunny Italy.'

The frame-story of the Parrot Tales, *split into three tales, was collected by the learned Giuseppe Pitrè, in Sicily, over a century ago, from peasant lips. Several versions have been found in Italy. The interest of this one, apart from its entertainment value, is the fact that, unlike most of the folktales of similar origins, it stems from the Sanskrit version, and not from an intermediate Islamic source, such as the Turkish, Arabic, or Persian collections. The medium through which a Sanskrit-based tale reached Europe is not known.*

I

Once upon a time there lived a king, who had an only daughter, who was the sun, moon, and stars to him. He gave her everything which she desired, and there was nothing in the world which she was denied.

On the day when this story begins, the King and the Princess went driving out into the countryside, as it was springtime. So many beautiful flowers were in every valley that they drove quite a long way. They stopped the royal coach, walked about for a while, and after picking a few blossoms, drove back to the palace.

Now, no sooner did the Princess return to the palace hall, than she saw with dismay that her favourite toy, a beautiful life-like doll, had been left behind somewhere – on a hedge, maybe. She was out of her mind with grief, for that doll had been hers since ever she could remember, and as she had no brothers or sisters, it was everything to her. The doll was dressed as she was, daily, and had almost as many jewels as the Princess herself possessed.

So she decided that, without telling her father, she would slip out at the first possible moment and go to look for the doll.

It was not long before the King went to change his robes, and she found her chance to escape through a secret exit. Not being very used to going about alone, however, the Princess was soon completely lost. Night was falling when she saw a fine palace in front of her. Knocking on the door, she shouted, 'Who is the owner of this magnificent building?' She called out in a most regal way, and the captain of the guard who was at the entrance said, 'Lady, this is the palace of the Great and Glorious King of Spain!'

'I am a king's daughter,' she said, and she was at once admitted, and taken to a guest chamber. There she was undressed by several maids, and robed for the night with much ceremony. She soon fell asleep, and without any fear, since she was in a royal household, slept as if she were safe at home.

Next morning, she was taken before the King of Spain.

He was very impressed with her appearance, and with her manner and charm.

'Will you remain here with me and administer the palace as if it were your own?' he asked, for he had no daughter, and his wife had been dead some years.

'Certainly, I shall be happy to do so,' said the Princess, and she soon felt that she had never lived anywhere else in the world.

But there was trouble in the palace among the courtiers. Twelve royal maidens who were related to the King of Spain by marriage felt that they had been passed over for a complete stranger.

Gossip and intrigue circulated and soon the courtiers had taken sides. Some were for the royal maidens, others were for the Princess.

'How can we take orders and instructions from one so young and inexperienced in our ways as this girl!' they whispered. 'Who indeed is she, though she says she is a true Princess? Let us plot her downfall!' So they went to her, and with smiles and giggles said, 'Oh, dear lady, why do you not come with us upon our next outing? There are many things we could show you, far away from the confines of the court!'

'Oh, no,' the Princess shook her head, 'I am not sure that I can go anywhere without the permission of dear Royal Papa. He never likes me to leave his side.'

'But we know a sure method by which you can be spared,' said they. 'Let us tell you what to say to His Majesty.'

'What am I to say?' cried the Princess.

'Just say "By the soul of your daughter you must let me go with the royal maidens!"' they murmured in her ear.

'Very well,' said the Princess, 'I will try it.' But no sooner had she said the fateful words to the devoted King, than the smile left his face, the light of anger came to his eyes, and he shouted, 'Ah! Wretched girl! How dare you speak to me like that! To the trapdoor with you!' And the unfortunate Princess felt herself propelled towards a large trapdoor in the floor. She soon was falling through time and space, falling, falling in the most horrible darkness.

Suddenly, she stopped falling, and could feel the wood of another door. She turned the knob, blindly, and it gave way. Then she felt tinder and matches in her hand, and lit a lamp. Another door stood half-open, and slowly advancing, the Princess saw in the light of the lamp a beautiful young girl, as fair as the moon on her fourteenth night. This unfortunate young creature had her hands bound and a silver padlock on her mouth, so that she could not speak. The Princess looked at her questioningly, and the girl indicated that, under the pillow, was a silver key. The Princess found it, and saw that it was set with a green stone in the top.

The Princess unlocked the girl's lips, and she said, 'I am a king's daughter, stolen away by a wicked magician. He had left me here for I do not know how long, and feeds me when he comes. Every night at midnight he arrives, with two slaves carrying bowls of food and fruit.'

'But, tell me,' said the Princess, 'is there any way in which you might be freed? This imprisonment must be torment for you!'

'I can only find that out by asking the magician,' said the other, 'so tonight conceal yourself under the bed, and listen to all that passes between us. I shall try to wheedle some sort of information regarding this out of him, so listen well, dear lady, and save me if you can.'

'That I shall do, with all my heart and all my strength, if it comes to that,' said the Princess, and she got under the bed in readiness for the arrival of the magician.

When twelve o'clock came, the door flew open, and a strange-looking man, with a long dark robe, white beard, and fierce, piercingly blue eyes appeared, attended by two coal-black slaves of savage aspect. The magician took the key, unlocked the younger Princess's lips and with every sign of affection, fed her with his own hands from the bowls.

While she was eating, he was paying her extravagant compliments, and she said, 'Now, just for argument's sake, if I were ever to escape from here, how could it be done? I pray you tell me, that I might be diverted by the telling of it!'

The magician looked taken aback for a few seconds; then he smiled and said: 'Well, since there is no chance that you ever *could* be able to do it, I will tell you.

'It would be necessary for someone to put gunpowder all around the palace; and, at midnight, when I appear, set light to it. Then it would blow a complete circle around the palace, and I would be blown up into the air. But eat these delicacies – you would not get food like this in the world except through my magical agency!'

The young girl laughed, and passed it off as

though the idea meant nothing to her. After that, the magician caused one of the slaves to wash her mouth with rosewater, the magician dried it himself with a fine napkin, and he went away, not forgetting to lock her lips again with the padlock.

After a short while, the Princess came out from under the bed and said, 'Sister, sister, have no fear, I will go and summon help from my adoptive father up there in the castle. Somehow you will be rescued, or we shall be blown up together!'

She crept out of the room, climbed through the trapdoor, and began to shout for the King of Spain.

The King of Spain, who had missed her after she had disappeared through the trapdoor at his command, came to her, and she told him the whole story from beginning to end.

He said, 'I will send for the captain of the guard, even though it be the middle of the night, to make a ring of gunpowder around the castle as soon as he possibly can get the men roused. I myself will light the powder at the very second twelve o'clock strikes. Leave it to me, and go back to your own room, my dear.'

'No, no, father,' cried the Princess, 'I have promised that poor girl that I shall rescue her, or we shall both get blown up together.'

'So be it,' said the King of Spain, and the brave Princess vanished again down the tunnel. She comforted the girl with the silver padlock on her lips, as well as she could, and whispered words of encouragement to help her pass the hours of waiting.

The King's sappers began digging, and worked away with a will to prepare the mine. The day passed very slowly for the two girls. By the time it was nearly midnight, the gunpowder was ready in one large circle all around the castle.

When the clock struck twelve midnight, the magician came as usual through the door of the chamber. The Princess was hidden under the bed, and the girl with the silver padlock on her lips looked as she always did, patiently waiting for him.

The torch set the gunpowder alight, the ring of powder ignited, and the magician was blown into the sky in a thousand pieces. The two girls were severely shocked for a few seconds; but soon began to laugh with joy and relief, though they had singed eyebrows, torn clothes and blackened faces.

When the King of Spain saw them, climbing out of the tunnel, he exclaimed, 'Ah, my beautiful daughter! Come to me and be with me here in harmony for the rest of our lives! You my dear,' he added to the brave Princess who had effected the rescue, 'You shall have the crown after I am dead!'

'No, no, dear King of Spain,' cried she, 'I am a king's daughter myself, and I, too, have right to a crown!'

So a feast was prepared which took many days and nights of jollity.

This matter spread all over the earth, everyone taking the story to his or her own country, and everybody talked of the great courage and goodness of that beautiful Princess who had saved another King's daughter from certain death and dishonour.

And all the chief actors in this tale (except, of course, the magician) enjoyed life and happiness in all the days of their sojourn in this world.

II

ONCE THERE WAS a king who had an only daughter who was as beautiful as any young girl ever born to humankind.

On her eighteenth birthday news came that the King of the Turks wanted to marry her.

'Oh, what do I want with a Turk for a husband?' she said, and refused to have anything to do with him.

Soon after this affair, she lapsed into a very unhappy state of health – she, who had never had anything wrong with her in her life before.

Her father the King sent for doctors from far and wide, but none could be found to help her, let alone to tell what was actually wrong with the Princess.

She lay on her silken sheets, eyes rolling, body shivering, her limbs twisted under her.

Her poor father was in distress, and called the wise men of his capital city together. 'My friends, hear me at this time of my personal distress as you did when the country was in danger from enemies,' he said. 'Tell me what I am to do!'

'Your Majesty,' said they in unison, 'find the Princess of whom we have just heard, who caused the rescue of the daughter of the King of Spain from the dreaded magician who hid her away and locked her lips. Find her, and she will find a way!' For the Princess who wrought the miracle had become the talk of every country in the world, and there was no quarter of the earth where her name was unknown.

The King ordered ships to set out that very hour to search for the lady. 'If the King of Spain will not let her leave him and come, then shall we go to war against Spain, though she be the mightiest country of Christendom!' spoke the monarch boldly, with eyes of fire.

The ships set off, and arrived off Spain very soon. All their guns blazed in salute across the bay, the envoy set foot on the earth of Spain, and bent down to kiss it in homage. 'A message, a message from a faraway king to the King of Spain,' was the cry.

The sealed letter borne by an envoy dressed in scarlet and gold, was handed to the King of Spain.

He broke the seal, and let his eye wander over the message. But he clenched his fist and shouted, 'I will go to war, but I will never send my dearest adopted daughter on such a mission!' and he tore up the letter.

The Princess came from behind the ivory screen and asked, 'What is it, Royal Papa? Who was that letter from, and what is this about?'

'Dear daughter, the King of another country has sent his ships to take you away to help in the affair of *his* daughter. You shall not go, I forbid it!'

'What are you afraid about? I will return to you, in time, after I have settled this thing,' she said.

So she went, after taking leave of him with great tenderness.

When she arrived, the King went to greet her.

'My daughter, if you cure this child of mine you shall have my crown!' he vowed.

'I am a king's daughter myself, and I already have a crown,' she said, as she had said to the other King. 'Let us see what the matter is, never mind about crowns or coronets.'

She was taken to the Princess's bedchamber and saw her lying there, all wasted away.

Now, after a few moments' thought, the Princess who had just arrived turned to the King and said, 'Your Majesty, have some soup made, and some chickens cooked. Also, cheese and fruit. Have these things brought to me here, and lock me in this room alone with your daughter for the space of three days.

'No matter what you hear, or even if I cry out for you to open up, do not do so. Within three days I will deliver your daughter to you alive or dead.

'Remember, whatever I say to you, do not open the door.'

Soon everything was done to her liking, and the great bolts were fastened on each side. But when she went to sit beside the Princess as the light from the windows failed, she discovered that they had forgotten the tinder to light the candles at night. So, she poked about in cupboards, with the unlit candle in her hand, looking for a tinder-box. One of the doors led to a small room; and, looking out of the window, she saw a light in the distance. She could not stand the dark, so she descended from the window with a ladder of silk to try to find the light.

When she got near the light she saw it was a huge black cauldron placed on a fire. There was a tall Turk stirring something in the pot with a stick.

She greeted him with, 'What are you doing, O Noble Turk?' And he replied, 'My King wanted the daughter of this King, but she did not want him, so he is having this done as a bewitchment.'

'Oh, poor Turk,' she said, laying her hand on his sleeve, 'you must be tired, stirring like that for so long and so bravely.'

'Yes,' said the Turk, 'I am rather tired now, and I wish that someone else would help me.'

'Why, I will help you,' said she. 'You just lie down there, and I will continue stirring for you.'

'That is extremely kind,' said the Turk, yawning, and he lay down. She took the stick and began to stir.

'Am I doing it correctly?' asked the Princess.

'Yes, indeed, beautiful lady,' the Turk replied. 'If only I could sleep for a little while…'

'Well, you take a sleep now and I will stir,' said she, and the Turk fell into a doze.

When he was asleep she bent down, and, with her amazing strength, threw him into the boiling cauldron. When she saw that he was dead, she lit her candle at the fire and returned up the silken ladder to the bedchamber.

She sat beside the sick Princess's bed, and saw that she seemed to be better. For three days and three nights she nursed her and fed her with the delicacies which the King had provided. When the Princess got up on the morning of the third day, perfectly well again, the girls embraced each other, and called through the door for the King to open it. He came in at once, and kissed them both with great joy.

'Ah, my daughter,' he said to the Princess who had wrought the miracle, 'I owe you my kingdom and my daughter's life What in the world can I give you to repay you? Tell me, I am at your command.'

'Nothing my gifts have brought me are of any value; I only work by the power vested in me by Providence,' she replied.

'Stay with us here,' pleaded the King, 'and you shall be as dear to me as my own daughter.'

'No, you threatened my father with war if I did not come, remember,' she said, 'and my father will declare war upon your country if I do not return at once, so let me go, with your leave.'

Sadly, the King agreed, and thanking her again, gave a great feast in her honour. Loaded with costly presents for herself and her father, she soon departed, and returned to the King of Spain's palace.

III

Once upon a time there lived a king and queen, who had a handsome son whose only diversion in life was to go hunting. Morning and noon he hunted, attended by many huntsmen. Now, one day, he was far afield when he saw a most beautiful doll lying on the ground. It was dressed like a real live princess would be attired, and even had real jewels in its ears and round its neck. He looked everywhere to see where the owner of this fabulous doll might be, but there was no one to be seen in any direction. So he took the doll up onto his horse, as if it had been a lady, and declared to the others, 'We shall return home at once now,' and they rode back to his father's kingdom. In his private room the Prince examined the doll, and placed it upon his mantelpiece, looking at it long. 'What a beautiful doll,' he said again and again to himself. 'If the doll is so beautiful, what must its mistress be like? Surely it is made in her image.' After he had taken the doll to his room the Prince would not leave it, gazing upon it fondly hour by hour, murmuring, 'Just think of the mistress, if the doll is so beautiful!'

When he had not seen the Prince for several days, and the court physician told him he had been keeping to his private apartment, the King went to see him. He found the Prince looking at the doll on the mantelpiece, muttering feverishly, 'If this is the doll, how beautiful must be the mistress!'

'My boy!' cried the King. 'Are you completely out of your wits! What are you doing with that image? Have you become an idol-worshipper in the space of a few days since you came back from your last hunt? Tell me the truth of the matter at once.'

The Prince turned lacklustre eyes upon his father and said in a low voice, 'If this is the doll, just think how beautiful the mistress of such a doll must be! Just think of the mistress, if this is only the doll!'

Horrified at his son's wasted appearance and strange manner, the King went back to the throne-room and summoned all his courtiers.

He said: 'See what has happened to my son, he has become mad! What is to be done? The physician says he has no physical ill, no fever, no broken bones, but his mind has completely gone. Such a man cannot possibly take my place as ruler when I am gone. What is to be done?'

One aged sage stepped forward and bowed before the throne.

'Speak,' said the King.

'Your Majesty, people are talking about a miraculous Princess who goes from kingdom to kingdom, curing people. She is said to have found the King of Spain's lost daughter, and to have cured another princess only recently. Send for her, and if she will not come, declare war upon her father!'

'Well said,' agreed the King. 'Send an envoy for her at once. I will brook no delay. My son must be cured for the sake of the country and the people, if not for mine.'

So a suitable courtier was sent with a long retinue and a sealed letter from the King.

When these foreigners arrived, the hall of audience was full of people thronging through it. The Princess looked from behind the carved screen and said to the King, who was reading the letter, 'What ails you, father?'

'Nothing, nothing my dear,' said the King, frowning and biting his nails, tossing the letter into the corner rolled up into a ball.

'There must be something wrong. Who are all these strangers at court, and what news does that foreign envoy bring in that letter which you have thrown away?' she asked gently.

'It is war,' said the King testily, 'unless I allow you to go on yet another of these ridiculous journeys to the far corners of the world!'

'Is someone ill again?' she asked.

'Yes, this time a young prince, who is behaving very strangely and seems to be quite out of his wits. I do not think that I should expose you to these dangers...' said the King.

'I must go, I shall soon come back, I promise, dear

father,' said she, and after he had embraced her, she set off.

With many attendants and soldiers, the Princess's journey took quite a time, but at last she arrived at the Prince's private room. He was looking at a beautiful doll and sighing deeply, murmuring to himself the while, 'Oh, what a beautiful doll. If this is the doll, just think how wonderful the mistress of this doll must be!' But as he was now so feeble, he said it all under his breath.

So the Princess said to the King: 'Close me up in this room with the Prince for three days. Lock the doors and do not come in until I call you to open them. Leave some food here for me to give him daily, and in three days I will bring him out alive and well, or dead.'

They did as she asked, and she sat with him, feeding him chicken broth sip by sip, until she made him stronger.

At last, when he was able he called in quite a loud voice: 'Oh, what a beautiful doll! If that is the doll, how much more beautiful must be the mistress!'

'Ah, wretch,' cried the Princess, 'so it is *you* who have got my doll!'

He raised himself on one elbow and said, 'Are you the owner of the doll?'

'Yes,' she said, 'I am. Now drink this chicken broth and get well.'

When he was able to get out of the bed, they called through the door to his father that he was cured.

So the King and the courtiers came in, and carried the Prince out to the people, happy and well, looking even more handsome than he had been before.

The Princess took down her doll from the mantelpiece, and hugged it for sheer joy.

Soon the Prince told her he was in love with her, and begged her to marry him. 'For though the doll is beautiful,' he said, 'you are so much more beautiful, as I knew you would be. Will you marry me and become in time the Queen, when I am King?'

And so she answered that she would.

The King, delighted to have such a wonderful daughter-in-law, gave her many jewels, and the people were wild with joy at having the famous Princess for their Prince's bride.

Several letters were written and sent with trusted messengers right away: among them one to the King of Spain to tell him that she would not be returned to him as a daughter, but later, she would go back with her Prince to pay their respects; and another letter to the King whose daughter she had cured.

At the time of the wedding, which was one of great splendour, all the monarchs came together and helped to make the Princess's good fortune complete. And she lived in great peace and happiness till the end of her days.

Dick Whittington and his Cat

The thrilling and romantic story of poor Dick Whittington and his rise to fame and fortune through the exploits of a cat which was his only possession, was first published three hundred and fifty years ago in London. It has remained a rags-to-riches epic ever since. Sir Richard Whittington did, in fact, exist; he was indeed three times Lord Mayor of London; he did marry a certain Alice Fitz-Warren. These, however, are the only three true facts of the story, so far as can be ascertained. He was not of humble birth; the son of Sir William Whittington of Gloucestershire, he was born in about 1358, almost two centuries before his highly coloured adventures first saw the light of day. And yet his biographer, Besant, seems to have believed the tale of the cat. Research has shown that the tale was current in Europe in the century before Whittington's birth. It is to be found attributed to a merchant of Genoa and two citizens of Venice, not to mention its fame in Portugal, Norway, Denmark, Russia, and France. The earliest form is the legend of the foundation of the royal house of Qays, written by Abdallah,

son of Fazlullah, of Shiraz, in Persia, sixty years before Dick Whittington's birth. He, in his turn, refers the events to the 11th century. This enthralling grafting of a popular story onto a real-life figure's history is supplied by the famous folklorist Andrew Lang, in this version, from the ancient chap-book version of Gomme and Wheatley.

Dick Whittington was a very little boy when his father and mother died; so little indeed that he never knew them, nor the place where he was born. He wandered about the country as ragged as a colt, till he met with a wagoner who was going to London, and who let him walk all the way by the side of his wagon without paying anything. This pleased little Whittington very much, as he wanted to see London badly, for he had heard that the streets were paved with gold, and he was willing to get a bushel of it. But how great was his disappointment, poor boy! when he saw the streets covered with dirt instead of gold, and found himself in a strange place, without a friend, without food, and without money.

Though the wagoner was so charitable as to let him walk up by the side of the wagon for nothing, he took good care not to know him when they came to town, and the poor boy was, in a little time, so cold and hungry that he wished himself in a good kitchen and by a warm fire in the country.

In this distress he asked charity of several people and one of them bid him, 'Go and work, you idle rogue.' 'That I will,' said Whittington, 'with all my heart; I will work for you if you will let me.'

The man, who thought this was wit and impertinence (though the poor lad intended only to show his readiness to work), gave him a blow with a stick which cut his head so that the blood ran down.

In this situation, and fainting for want of food, he laid himself down at the door of one Mr Fitzwarren, a merchant, where the cook saw him. Being an ill-natured hussy, she said that if he did not go about his business, she would throw boiling water on him. At this time Mr Fitzwarren came home, and also began to scold the poor boy, telling him to go to work.

Whittington answered that he would be glad to work if anybody would employ him, and that he should be able if he could get some food to eat, for he had had nothing for three days, and he was a poor country boy, and knew nobody, and nobody would employ him.

He then tried to get up, but he was so very weak that he fell down again. The merchant was sorry for him, and he ordered the servants to take him in and give him some meat and drink; and to let him help the cook to do any dirty work that she had to give him. People are too apt to accuse those who beg of being idle, but give themselves no concern to put them in the way of getting something to do, or considering whether they are able to do it, which is not charity.

But we return to Whittington, who would have lived happily in this worthy family had he not been bumped about by the cross cook, who was always roasting or basting, and who, when she had nothing else to do, used to smack poor Whittington! At last Miss Alice, his master's daughter, was told about it and she took pity on the poor boy, and made the servants treat him kindly.

Besides the crossness of the cook, Whittington had another difficulty to get over before he could be happy. He had, by order of his master, a bed placed for him in an attic, where there were a number of rats and mice. They often ran over the poor boy's nose and disturbed him in his sleep. After some time, however, a gentleman who came to his master's house gave Whittington a penny for brushing his shoes. This he put into his pocket, being determined to use it to the best advantage; and the next day, seeing a woman in the street with a cat under her arm, he ran up to know the price of it. As the cat was a good mouser, the woman asked a great deal of money for it. But on Whittington's telling her he had but a penny in the world, and that he wanted a cat badly, she let him have it.

This cat Whittington concealed in his room, for fear she should be beat about by his mortal enemy the cook, and here she soon killed or frightened away the rats and mice, so that the poor boy could now sleep as sound as a top.

Soon after this the merchant, who had a ship ready to sail, called for his servants, as his custom was, so that each of them might venture something to try their luck; and whatever they sent was to pay neither freight nor custom, for he thought justly that God

Almighty would bless him the more for his readiness to let the poor partake of his fortune.

All the servants appeared except poor Whittington, who, having neither money nor goods, could not think of sending anything to try his luck; but his good friend Miss Alice, thinking his poverty kept him away, ordered him to be called.

She then offered to lay down something for him, but the merchant told his daughter that would not do, it must be something of his own. Upon which poor Whittington said he had nothing but a cat which he had bought for a penny that was given him. 'Fetch the cat, boy,' said the merchant, 'and send her.' Whittington brought poor puss and delivered her to the captain, with tears in his eyes, for he said he should now be disturbed by the rats and mice as much as ever. All the company laughed at the adventure except Miss Alice, who pitied the poor boy, and gave him something to buy another cat.

While puss was beating the billows at sea, poor Whittington was severely beaten at home by his mistress, the cook, who used him so cruelly, and made such fun of him for sending his cat to sea, that at last the poor boy decided to run away and, having packed up the few things he had, he set out very early in the morning on All-Hallows Day. He travelled as far as Holloway, and there sat down on a stone to consider what course he should take; but while he was thinking, Bow bells, of which there were only six, began to ring; and he thought their sounds addressed him in this manner:

'Turn again, Whittington,
Thrice Lord Mayor of London.'

'Lord Mayor of London!' said he to himself; 'what would one not endure to be Lord Mayor of London, and ride in such a fine coach? Well, I'll go back again, and bear all the pummelling and ill-usage of Cicely rather than miss the opportunity of being Lord Mayor!' So home he went, and happily got into the house and back to his work before Mrs Cicely made her appearance.

We must now follow Miss Puss to the coast of Africa. How perilous are voyages at sea, how uncertain the winds and the waves, and how many accidents attend a naval life!

The ship which had the cat on board was long beaten at sea, and at last, by contrary winds, driven on a part of the coast of Barbary which was inhabited by Moors unknown to the English. These people received our countrymen with civility; and therefore the captain, in order to trade with them, showed them samples of the goods he had on board, and sent some of them to the King of the country, who was so well pleased that he sent for the captain and Mr.

Fitzwarren's agent to his palace, which was about a mile from the sea. Here they were placed, according to the custom of the country, on rich carpets, flowered with gold and silver. The King and Queen being seated at the upper end of the room, dinner was brought in, which consisted of many dishes. But no sooner were the dishes put down but an amazing number of rats and mice came from all directions and gobbled up all the meat in an instant.

The agent, in surprise, turned round to the nobles and asked if these vermin were not offensive. 'Oh, yes,' said they, 'very offensive; and the King would give half his treasure to be freed of them, for they not only destroy his dinner, as you see, but they attack him in his room, and even in bed, so that he is obliged to be watched while he is sleeping for fear of them.'

The agent jumped for joy; he remembered poor Whittington and his cat, and told the King that he had a creature on board ship that would get rid of all these vermin immediately. The King's heart heaved so high at the joy which this news gave him that his turban dropped off his head. 'Bring this creature to me,' said he; 'vermin are dreadful in a court, and if she will perform what you say I will load your ship with gold and jewels in exchange for her.' The agent, who knew his business, took this opportunity to set forth the merits of Miss Puss. He told His Majesty that it would be inconvenient to part with her, as when she was gone, the rats and mice might destroy the goods in the ship – but to oblige his Majesty he would fetch her. 'Run, run,' said the Queen; 'I am impatient to see the dear creature.'

Away flew the agent, while another dinner was provided, and returned with the cat just as the rats and mice were devouring that also. He immediately put down Miss Puss, who killed a great number of them.

The King rejoiced greatly to see his old enemies destroyed by so small a creature, and the Queen was highly pleased, and desired the cat might be brought near that she might look at her. Upon which the factor called 'Pussy, pussy, pussy!' and she came to him. He then presented her to the Queen, who started back, and was afraid to touch a creature who had made such a havoc among the rats and mice; however, when the man stroked the cat and called 'Pussy, pussy!' the Queen also touched her and cried 'Putty, putty!' for she had not learned English.

He then put the cat down on the Queen's lap, where she, purring, played with her Majesty's hand and then sang herself to sleep.

The King having seen the exploits of Miss Puss, and being informed that her kittens would stock the whole country, bargained with the captain and factor for the whole ship's cargo, and then gave them ten times as much for the cat as all the rest amounted to. On which, taking leave of their Majesties and other great personages at court, they sailed with a fair wind for England – whither we must now attend them.

The morning had scarcely dawned when Mr Fitzwarren arose to count over the cash and settle the business for that day. He had just entered the counting-house and seated himself at the desk, when somebody came tap, tap, at the door. 'Who's there?' said Mr Fitzwarren. 'A friend,' answered the other. 'What friend can come at this unseasonable time?' 'A real friend is never unseasonable,' answered the other. 'I come to bring you good news of your ship Unicorn.' The merchant bustled up in such a hurry that he forgot his gout, instantly opened the door, and who should be seen waiting but the captain and agent, with a cabinet of jewels, and a bill of lading, for which the merchant lifted up his eyes and thanked heaven for sending him such a prosperous voyage. Then they told him the adventures of the cat, and showed him the cabinet of jewels which they had brought for Mr Whittington. Upon which he cried out with great earnestness, but not in the most poetical manner:

'Go, send him in, and tell him of his fame,
And call him Mr Whittington by name.'

Mr Fitzwarren was a good man; for when some who were present told him that this treasure was too much for such a poor boy as Whittington, he said:

'God forbid that I should deprive him of a penny. It is his own, and he shall have it to a farthing.' He then ordered Mr Whittington in, who was at this time cleaning the kitchen and would have excused himself from going into the counting-house, saying the room was swept and his shoes were dirty and full of hobnails. The merchant, however, made him come in, and ordered a chair to be set for him. Upon which, thinking they intended to make fun of him, as had been too often the case in the kitchen, he begged his master not to mock a poor simple fellow, who intended no harm, but let him go about his business. The merchant, taking him by the hand, said: 'Indeed, Mr Whittington, I sent for you to congratulate you on your great success. Your cat has made you more money than I am worth in the world, and may you long enjoy it and be happy!'

At length, being shown the treasure, and convinced by then that all of it belonged to him, he fell upon his knees and thanked the Almighty for his providential care of such a poor and miserable creature. He then laid all the treasure at his master's feet, who refused to take any part of it, but told him he hoped the wealth would be a comfort to him, and would make him happy. He then applied to his mistress, and to his good friend, Miss Alice, who refused to take any part of the money, but told him she heartily rejoiced at his good success, and wished him all imaginable happiness. He then gave presents to the captain, the agent and the ship's crew for the care they had taken of his cargo. He likewise distributed presents to all the servants of the house, not forgetting even his old enemy the cook, though she little deserved it.

After this Mr Fitzwarren advised Mr Whittington to send for the necessary people and dress himself like a gentleman, and made him the offer of his house to live in till he could provide himself with one better.

Now it came to pass when Mr Whittington's face was washed, his hair curled and he was dressed in a rich suit of clothes, that he turned out a genteel young fellow; and as wealth contributes much to give a man confidence, he in a little time dropped that sheepish behaviour which was mainly caused by a depression of spirits, and soon grew a sprightly and good companion, and Miss Alice, who had formerly pitied him, now fell in love with him.

When her father saw that they had this liking for each other he suggested that they should marry. The Lord Mayor, Court of Aldermen, Sheriffs, the Company of Stationers, the Royal Academy of Arts and a number of eminent merchants attended the ceremony, and were elegantly treated at an entertainment made for that purpose.

History further relates that they lived very happily, had several children, and died at a good old age. Mr. Whittington served Sheriff of London and was three times Lord Mayor. In the last year of his mayoralty he entertained King Henry V and his Queen, after his conquest of France, upon which occasion the King, in consideration of Whittington's merit, said: 'Never had a prince such a subject'; which being told to Whittington at the table, he replied: 'Never had a subject such a King.' His Majesty out of respect to his good character, conferred the honour of knighthood on him soon after.

Sir Richard many years before his death constantly fed a great number of poor citizens, built a church and a college to it, with a yearly allowance for poor scholars, and near it erected a hospital.

He also built Newgate Prison, and gave liberally to St Bartholomew's Hospital and other public charities.

Don't Count Your Chickens

This tale is the origin of perhaps the best-known proverb in the world – 'The Girl and the Pitcher of Milk'. Professor Max Muller remarks how the tale has survived the rise and fall of empires and the change of languages, and the perishing of works of art, and stresses the attraction whereby 'this simple children's tale should have lived on and maintained its place of honour and its undisputed sway in every schoolroom of the East and every nursery of the West'.

In the Eastern versions, it is always a man who is the fantasist and whose hopes come to grief; in the West, it is almost always a woman. The man generally imagines that he will marry and have a son, while the woman tends to think of riches and marriage.

The outline is invariably the same: details change. In the Hindu tale (in the Hitopadesa*), flour is spilt; in La Fontaine's French fable, it is milk. Truhana, of the medieval Spanish* Don Lucanor *(given here) finds the honey coming to grief; in the Arabic of the Kalila, it is butter and honey. The*

Turkish Forty Vizirs *collection – and the Greek of Symeon features oil and honey; in Aesop it is eggs which are smashed; in the* Arabian Nights, *glass.*

Emphases of the meaning vary. With the Brahmin, it is greed and lack of foresight, with the Persian devotee in the Turkish, undue concentration on one thing; in the Arabian Kalila *and elsewhere, there is a hint that violent action is one's undoing. Rabelais (in his* Gargantua*) attributes this folly to a shoemaker who struck a pot of milk in his excitement at becoming rich in fantasy: 'Destroying that which may lead to success by the thought of that success itself.'*

Once upon a time there lived a woman called Truhana. Not being very rich, she had to go yearly to the market to sell honey, the precious product of her hive.

Along the road she went, carrying the jar of honey upon her head, calculating as she walked the money she would get for the honey. 'First,' she thought, 'I will sell it, and buy eggs. The eggs I shall set under my fat brown hens, and in time there will be plenty of little chicks. These in turn will become chickens, and from the sale of these, lambs could be bought.'

Truhana then began to imagine how she could become richer than her neighbours, and look forward to marrying well her sons and daughters.

Trudging along, in the hot sun, she could see her fine sons and daughters-in-law, and how the people would say that it was remarkable how rich she had become, who was once so poverty-stricken.

Under the influence of these pleasurable thoughts, she began to laugh heartily, and preen herself, when, suddenly, striking the jar with her hand, it fell from her head and smashed upon the ground. The honey became a sticky mess upon the ground.

Seeing this, she was as cast down as she had been excited, on seeing all her dreams lost for illusion.

The Hawk and the Nightingale

The origination of fables has been claimed for the Jews (Solomon is reputed to have composed two or three thousand of them), the Greeks, the Indians and the Egyptians. Aesop is said to have lived in the 6th century BC, but there are indications of fables in Egyptian papyri of 800 to 1000 years earlier. Jotham's apologue of the trees who desired a king was for long thought to be the oldest, but the Hebrew Book of Judges, *in which it is found, dates in its present form only from about the 3rd century BC.*

'The Hawk and the Nightingale', given here, is from the works of the Greek poet Hesiod, who flourished about 800 BC. It has been regarded by many as the earliest complete fable traceable to a literary work. It has been attributed to Aesop and others, but Hesiod is the earliest source. It certainly seems like the prototype of 'A bird in the hand is worth two in the bush'.

A NIGHTINGALE WAS sitting alone among the shady branches of an oak tree. She sang with so melodious and trilling a voice that the woods echoed with her song.

A hawk, perched not far away, was searching the woods for something to catch. No sooner had he found the tiny songster than he swooped, caught her in his talons, and told her to prepare for death.

'Oh!' said she, 'do not do anything so barbarous and so unbecoming as to kill me. Remember, I never did anything wrong – and I would only be a mouthful for such a one as you. Why do you not attack some larger bird, which would be a braver thing to do and would give you a better meal, and let me go?'

'Yes,' said the hawk, 'you may try to persuade me if you can. But I had not found any prey today until I saw you. And now you want me to let you go in hope of something better! But if I did, who would be the fool?'

Cecino the Tiny

Tom Thumb is the English version of Grimm's 19th century 'Thumblin' and of Perrault's 'Petit Pucet', published almost two hundred years before. The first printed version appeared in London, told by Richard Johnson, in 1621. Tom is supposed to have been the favourite dwarf of King Arthur, but we only hear of this a thousand years after Arthur's supposed date of death. Several cognates and parallels of the tale exist, in Germany, Denmark, South Europe and India, in which the tiny fellow has many and varied adventures. Like other peasant tales, the one given here ignores morality (Cecino joins a robber band, his father kills all his brothers) and the happy ending – Cecino drowns, and that is that. This kind of structure, in which anything can happen without need for didactic, is perhaps inherent in the fantasy origins of the story: a chickpea becomes a person, so he really is not anyone at all. The following version was collected from the oral tradition in 19th century Tuscany.

ONCE THERE LIVED a poor ignorant carpenter and his wife, who had always prayed for children, but had never been sent any by the Almighty.

When the husband came back from his daily work at the shop where he was sewing and hammering making tables and cupboards, he did nothing but make his poor wife's life a misery by saying that it was all her fault that they had no children in their long married life.

The woman was very sad about this and tried every way she could think of to conceive. She lit many candles in church, made pilgrimages to special places taken to be sure cures for barren women, ate certain herbs, and also gave her husband many magic philtres.

But to no avail. They could not make children, and each blamed the other, till they made each night a hell upon earth, quarrelling till dawn.

The carpenter began to spend more and more time at his shop, carving and hammering away at more and more cupboards and chests; the wife lit more candles than she could afford, and said her prayers so often that she was mumbling all the time under her breath, until people began to avoid her, thinking her to be a witch.

Life was not happy for either of them, and daily they grew further and further apart, and the carpenter was seriously thinking of leaving her and going away to some other place to start all over again.

One day, a poor-looking old woman knocked at the door of the humble house and asked for charity. The carpenter's wife said: 'I cannot give you anything, for I have spent all we can spare on candles, and having masses said so that we may have a child, someday, if God wills,' she whimpered.

'Give me something, however mean, and you shall have many sons,' promised the old woman, who had nose and chin meeting on her face.

'Good,' said the wife, 'I will give you all I can find, then.' And she went to look in the larder. Coming back a few moments later, she handed the old woman with the nutcracker face a brown loaf. 'Will this do?' she asked. 'It is all I can spare, honestly. There is nothing else in the house today.'

'Wonderful,' said the old woman. 'You can give me another when you get sons.'

'May it be so, in the name of the Almighty!' said the carpenter's wife piously. 'Even one will do.'

'You shall have many, my dear. Now I will go home and give my poor old husband something to eat, with this brown loaf,' said the crone, and went away, putting the loaf in her bag.

The carpenter's wife went about all day very happily at her daily work, singing, and wondered when she would have her first child.

The old woman went home, fed her old husband,

and took a small bag containing a hundred chickpeas back to the carpenter's wife. 'For the alms you have given me,' she said, 'you shall have many sons, as I promised. Put these hundred peas in a kneading-trough, and tomorrow they will become as many sons as there are peas.'

The carpenter's wife laughed, and thought that the old woman must be mad. 'How in the world can peas turn into children?' she screeched. 'You said I would have children! Can I not have them in the usual way?'

'No, this is the quickest way for you to have them,' said the old woman with nose and chin touching, and went away.

The wife of the carpenter said to herself, 'Well, maybe the old creature is a witch, and there may be something in it. I will do as she says; funnier things have happened. If by any chance this is the way to have children quickly and I miss the opportunity, my husband will give me a terrible scolding.' So she took the peas, put them in a kneading-trough and waited for the sons the woman had promised her.

That night the husband came home having drunk more wine than usual, and abused his wife, saying: 'Move over you barren cow, and let me get some peace and quiet in my own home!' She had never said a word, but under her breath she muttered: 'Just you wait until tomorrow, you will see something extraordinary indeed! Just you wait!'

'What are you mumbling about, silly creature?' grumbled the husband. 'Mumbling those prayers all night, you get on my nerves. One of these days I'll leave you, just you see if I don't!'

Then he fell into a drunken slumber.

The next morning the hundred peas had turned into one hundred lusty young sons.

'Papa, papa, give me a drink of water!' cried one, 'Mama, mama, give me some bread!' screamed another. Another cried: 'Pick me up!' Yet another: 'I want to go for a walk!' 'Papa, papa, make me a paper windmill!' demanded a fifth, and so it went on for about an hour.

The bad-tempered carpenter had had enough of this at such an early hour in the morning, so he took up a stick and began to beat the chickpea children. Soon he had killed them all, except one, who ran into the bedroom and hid away.

After the carpenter had gone to the shop, the unfortunate wife said to herself, crossly: 'Oh, devil take the man, he complained about my not having children, and now I've had them, he has killed them all! Is there no justice in the world? I wish I were dead!'

Then the pea which had escaped called, 'Mama, don't say that, I am here! I will look after you!'

The carpenter's wife could scarcely believe her eyes and ears, and she cried, 'How did you manage to escape, my son? What a miracle this is, indeed!'

'Has Papa gone?' asked the child. 'Yes,' said she, then, 'How are you named?' and he said, 'My name is Cecino, Mama.'

'What a nice name,' she said. 'Now, you must go to the shop and take your father's dinner to him, to save me going today, for I feel very tired; I had a sleepless night.'

'Yes, you must put the basket on my head,' said the boy, 'and I will carry it to Papa.'

The carpenter's wife, when the meal was ready, put the basket on the child's head and sent him off with the dinner. When he was near the shop, he began to cry: 'Oh, Papa, come and see, I am bringing your dinner.' Then the carpenter said to himself, 'Drat it, did I not kill them all?' Aloud he said, 'How did you escape when I killed all your brothers?'

'Oh, I hid under the handle of the pitcher,' said the pea child, 'and I survived.'

'Oh what a clever boy you are!' said the carpenter. 'You must go around among the country people and ask at all the houses whether they have anything to mend.'

'Very well,' said the boy, and the carpenter put him in his pocket. While he walked along the country road, the boy did nothing but chatter, and every person he met said that the carpenter must be mad, because they did not know it was the boy in his pocket who was talking.

When he saw some countrymen he asked, 'Have you anything which I can mend for you? I am a good carpenter, I can assure you.' They answered, 'Yes, we have something to be mended, but we cannot let you do it, for you are known to be mad.'

'Mad?' said he. 'Mad? I have never been taken for mad before, nor have any of my relatives ever been mad! I am wiser than you, I tell you. Why do you say I am mad?'

'Because you do nothing but talk to yourself on the road,' said they. 'Everybody has noticed it, lately. How do we know you can mend things properly if you are mad?'

'I was talking to my son,' said the carpenter, furiously. 'It is you who are unjust.'

'Where is your son?' they asked.

'In my pocket, of course!' he shouted in reply.

'That's a funny place to keep your son,' they said, sneeringly.

'Very well, I will show him to you,' said the carpenter and he took Cecino with his two fingers and placed him upon the palm of his hand to show him off to them.

'Oh what an amazing thing,' they cried. 'You must sell him to us!'

'Sell my son? What are you talking about?' said the carpenter. '*I* sell you my son, who is so valuable to me?' He put the boy on the horns of an ox and said, 'Wait for me there, my boy, I will go to that house and ask if they have any work for me.' So the boy said, 'I will wait here for you, Papa.'

Now two thieves passed by, and seeing the ox and its brother standing alone, said, 'Let us steal these oxen there with no one to look after them. Come!'

Then Cecino called out as loudly as he could, 'Look out, Papa, two thieves are going to steal the oxen!'

'Where does that voice come from?' the thieves asked each other, and they went near to the oxen and saw the miniature boy on the horn of one of them, as the carpenter hurried back to the cart.

'What have we here?' said one of the thieves, to the carpenter. 'You must let us buy him, whoever he is. We have found a rare creature for certain, and one that could be very useful to us!'

'No, no,' said the carpenter. 'What would his mother say if I sold him? I cannot do it.'

'We will give you as much money as you wish,' said the thieves. 'Just tell his mother that he died on the way home, of some accident. It will be quite easy, just try it.'

They tempted him so much that at last he gave the boy to them for a sack of gold.

They took Cecino, put him in a pocket and went away.

Then they went to the king's stable and wondered

if they could steal a fine horse or two from there. 'Do not betray us, now,' they warned Cecino, 'or it will be the worse for you.'

'Don't worry,' said Cecino, 'I will not betray you.'

The thieves came back with three fine Arab steeds which they had easily stolen while there were no royal grooms about. They took them home and put them in their own stable.

Afterwards, they went to Cecino, and said: 'Go, feed the horses, give them some oats, we are feeling too tired.' So Cecino was soon feeding the horses, but he fell into a bran dish and a black horse swallowed him.

When he did not return, the thieves went to look for him, but there was no sign of the tiny boy. 'He must have fallen asleep somewhere in the hay,' they said and went to look for him everywhere. 'Cecino, Cecino,' they called, 'where are you?'

'Inside the black horse,' cried Cecino.

So they killed the black horse, but Cecino was not there. 'Cecino, no tricks now, where are you?' they called. 'Inside the bay horse!' came the cry, so they killed the bay horse, but he was not in its stomach.

'Cecino, Cecino!' the thieves called out once more. 'Where are you?' but this time there was no reply. 'A great pity,' they said. 'That child would have been very useful indeed to us, and think of what we paid for him!'

Then they dragged the two horses which they had

cut open into a field.

A ravenously hungry wolf came loping past, and saw the two dead horses. 'I *will* have a good meal,' said he, his tongue lolling out hungrily, and he ate and ate, managing to swallow Cecino at the same time. The little boy had been in one of the horses all the time, but the thieves had missed seeing him because he was so small. Then the wolf became hungry again, and said to itself, 'I shall go and eat a goat this time; all that horsemeat has given me too much wind.'

When Cecino heard the wolf talking about eating a goat, circling the field where the goatherd was sitting, he called out at the top of his voice:

'Goatherd, goatherd, the wolf is coming to eat your goats! Beware!'

The goatherd began to throw stones at the wolf, and it ran and ran until it became sick, and Cecino was free once more. He hid under a large rock, beside which some robbers were counting a sum of money.

One of them said: 'Now we will divide this bag of money here, as we are far from anywhere, and no one will see us. You others be quiet whilst I am counting, or I shall kill you!'

They kept very still and silent, for they did not want to die, and the robber who was counting had a very sharp knife and a bad reputation for killing without asking questions first.

He began to count: 'One, two, three, four, and

five,' he said. Cecino then started to repeat the robber's words: 'One, two, three, four, and five!'

'I told you *not* to speak while I am counting!' shouted the angry robber. 'Keep still, or I will kill you!' Once more he began counting. 'One, two, three, four, and five!' and Cecino imitated him again, as loud as he was able.

'All right, then, you have asked for it!' roared the robber and plunged his knife into the heart of the one he thought was imitating him. 'Now we shall see if any of you speaks,' he said, and wiped his blade on his handkerchief. The counting continued, the robber beginning again: 'One, two, three, four, and five!'

As he got to the last number Cecino once more chimed in with 'One, two, three, four, and five!' as loud as he was able.

'Take care!' bellowed the killer, 'if you say anything again I shall have to finish you off!'

'Do you think I want to be killed?' cried the other robber. 'Carry on counting, I swear I will not speak.'

But the moment the counting began again, Cecino squeaked out the number of gold coins being counted, and the robber with the knife accounted for the second of his companions.

When he was wiping his knife again on his kerchief, Cecino began to count. 'There *is* someone else here, after all!' said the robber to himself, 'and I will be apprehended,' so he dropped the bag of gold and ran for his life.

When Cecino saw that he was alone, he came out, and saw the two dead robbers, and the bag of gold lying there unattended. He managed to get the bag onto his head, and walked home with it.

When he got near to his parents' house he called out: 'Mama, Papa, look what I have brought you! Come out and meet me!'

When the carpenter's wife heard him calling, she went out to meet him, and took the money, saying: 'Take care now, that you do not drown in these puddles of rainwater. I will put this gold carefully away for you, my son.'

The woman went home, to tell her husband how clever Cecino had been. She looked around for a moment to see if he was following, but could not see him. She got her husband, and they went searching for him everywhere. At last they found poor Cecino drowned in a puddle of rainwater, as his mother had feared would be his fate.

Her Lover's Heart

If the published record is to be credited, young Mrs Butler of London was unwittingly fed her lover's heart by her cruel husband, on or about the 6th June, 1707. The public print of the time adds a wealth of circumstantial detail, which may be intended to add plausibility to the account. The lady was, for example, an heiress, from Hackney Boarding School; her admirer was a rich Mr Perpont (of Fenchurch Street) who had fallen at the Battle of Almanza, in Spain.

Readers of Boccaccio in Britain might well have been surprised that history was repeating itself so near to home: for the Italian writer had reproduced almost exactly the same series of events, from a French troubadour's account dating to six hundred years before the alleged scandal at Hackney. On that occasion, the Lord de Couci's heart had been, equally inadvertently, consumed by the Lady du Fayel, after he had gone off to die in Palestine. He fell at the siege of Acre, in 1191. Thus runs the ninth story of the Fourth Day of the Decameron.

But even the gruesome feasts of France and England

are startlingly foreshadowed, again in striking detail, by the experience of the hapless Princess Kokla in 78 AD. She ate the heart of Prince Hodi of the Afghan frontier, according to 'every bard of the Punjab' – as General James Abbot discovered when he actually located her memorial statue in 1848. The chief material difference from the other narratives seems to be that the Indian lady ate both the heart and liver, roasted for her by her husband, Raja Rasalu, a traditional hero in North India.

World tales have a habit of appearing again and again in the work of the great writers, almost as if there is something irresistibly archetypal about them.

From the bards of the ancient Punjab to the Troubadours and Crusaders, to Boccaccio and popular eighteenth-century English reading, the 'Lover's Heart' theme surfaced again in the words of – Somerset Maugham.

On his 90th birthday, the great writer related a version of the story to his nephew Robin, calling it 'a pretty little tale'. This was on January 26, 1964: exactly one thousand, eight hundred and eighty-six years after our first tracing of the recital, in the Indian history – or legend – of Prince Hodi and Princess Kokla.

MANY, MANY YEARS ago, there was a great prince and hunter, whose name is still remembered as a man of skill and cunning, and whose adventures are sung throughout the land of India. He was Raja Rasalu, and he was married to the beautiful Princess, Rani Kokla. They lived in a splendid palace surrounded by beautiful gardens, a true abode for a king.

Rasalu used to go out hunting and, after pursuing the fleet-footed deer on his wonderful steed Fuladi – which means 'steely' – he would shoot one animal and bring back venison for his lady and feed it to her.

One day she said: 'If I go with you on the hunt, the deer will come to me, for I have eaten so much of their meat that they will feel an affinity with me.'

The Raja agreed to take her along, and, sure enough, when the Rani seated herself in the forest, the deer crowded around, as if fascinated. One of them, their leader, who was a great blue buck named Luddan, was so overcome that (in spite of his mate's warning) he ran to Kokla and threw himself at her feet.

Now the Raja cut off his ears and his tail as trophies, and let him go, but the buck swore vengeance, and he thought of a plan to punish Kokla the deer-eater.

He made his way to the palace of another prince, the Raja Hodi, and began to wander and cavort in his gardens, eating the fruits and trampling the grass. Raja Hodi came out to kill Luddan, and the buck ran away, luring him by degrees to the palace of Rani Kokla. As he approached, he saw the wonderful gardens and the splendid castle, and then he saw the Princess herself on the flat rooftop, walking arrayed in her finery. He called up to her, and she was attracted to him.

After an exchange of conversation and poems, she invited him into her apartments. The mynah bird which had been left on guard tried to stop him, and told another guard-bird, a parrot, that they should inform their master, Prince Rasalu, that a strange man had been allowed into the castle.

The birds protested to the Rani, but she scolded them, saying that nothing wrong was being done, entertaining a traveller was, after all, quite a normal thing to do. Then, in her rage, Kokla took the mynah and wrung her neck.

The parrot, however, was more crafty. Instead of reproaching the Princess, he said: 'Princess, you were right to punish this bird for her insolence! Let me out of my cage, and I shall peck her, just to show my own displeasure!'

The Rani opened the door of the cage. The parrot pecked the mynah, and then flew away. Seeing this, Prince Hodi became afraid. Embracing Kokla hastily, he fled to his own palace and threw himself on his bed, weeping bitterly for the loss of Kokla.

After looking everywhere in the forest, the parrot

came upon his master Rasalu, and told him what had happened. Rasalu mounted Fuladi and rode him at top speed to his palace, while a plan formed in his mind.

The Rani was lying asleep when Rasalu arrived home. He at once told Shadi, his parrot: 'Fly to the Princess's couch. Take the ring from her finger without waking her. Then speed to Prince Hodi's palace with it and inform him that I, Rasalu, have been killed by a fall in the woods, and that the Princess awaits him. Say that the ring is proof that the message is indeed from her!'

Shadi flew with all haste to Hodi's palace, and told him what he had been instructed to say. Hodi sprang upon his horse and was soon at Rasalu's gate. Rasalu himself came out and asked him what he wanted.

'I was passing by,' stuttered Hodi, 'and seeing this magnificent place thought I would look at it…'

'Pray come in,' said Rasalu, 'for a guest must be treated as such.'

Hodi could not refuse, for fear of arousing suspicion.

As he dismounted, Rasalu called out: 'Now die, faithless and dishonourable one!' He drew his sword and sliced right through Hodi, from head to toe. So sharp and thin was his wondrous sword that Hodi did not even feel the impact. In fact, he called out: 'You have not touched me, and I shall have my revenge!'

'Just move but one inch,' cried Rasalu, 'and you

will see!' Sure enough, as soon as Hodi moved, he split in two, along the line of the sword-cut.

Now Rasalu took out Hodi's liver and heart, saying, 'Kokla shall have venison today such as she has never had before!'

The Princess was still asleep. Rasalu quickly cooked the heart and liver and carried it to her. As she ate it, she said, 'I have never tasted anything so delicious as this, my own dear love, which you have killed and cooked for me with your own sweet hands...'

'So it should taste to you,' answered Raja Rasalu, 'for it is the flesh of your lover, eat as much as you will...'

Giving an agonised cry of the greatest anguish, the Rani ran to the turret of the castle and prepared to jump. As she looked down, she saw the body of Hodi lying there. Such was her grief that she was dead before she reached the ground, throwing herself from that towering height.

Rasalu, for his part, was staggering with shock. He descended to the bottom of the precipice upon which the castle was built, and kissed the lips of his beloved Kokla for the last time. Then, aware of the affinity which there was between the Princess and Hodi, he placed a cloth over the two of them and buried them, side by side, in the nearby ravine. He was utterly lonely for the rest of his days.

The New Hand

This story is very widely dispersed – from southern Europe to Scandinavia, and is also found in Britain and the United States. The 'New Hand' is often taken to be Jesus, who both works miracles and teaches people to avoid pride. It is found among the Gypsies, who may have helped to carry it to Russia, Sicily and elsewhere, from the Middle East. The tale is similar to many unofficial legends of Jesus current in Palestine. The following is adapted from the recital of Dick Brown, a Virginian at Sand Mountain, Alabama, taken down by the American J P Suverkrop in 1871. The Brothers Grimm have a famous nineteenth-century version, 'The Old Man Made Young Again', but the tale is certainly centuries old.

THERE WAS ONCE a sawmill on the edge of a wood, not far from here in Alabama, with the running river turning the wheel. An old black man, and a very fine man he was, owned the mill. But his son, named Sam, was quite unlike his father, lazy and useless he was. His father had to work hard to keep things going.

One day a stranger came along to the mill, a poor-looking fellow, who said that he would like to learn saw-milling, and that if he could be taught he would work for a year for nothing. The old man was glad to have his help, and young Sam thought that it was all right, too, because then he could shift some of his own work onto the New Hand. So the New Hand started, toting boards and doing chores around the place.

The owner liked the New Hand very much, and always gave him whatever he had himself. But Sam used to push the New Hand around, behind his father's back. When the old man caught Sam bossing and abusing the New Hand – and it happened several times – he punished him properly.

The day came when an old man came to collect a load of planks, and he was groaning with a bad back, and wishing that he was young and spry as he used to be. Then up spoke the New Hand, and he said to Sam and his father:

'If both of you go into the woods where you cannot see what is happening, leaving this man with me, and wait until I call you, I will make him as good as new again. But you must promise not to look, otherwise something bad will happen.'

So they promised, and the old man and his son went into the woods until they could not see what was happening at the mill. The New Hand said to the man with the bad back: 'Go and lie down on the saw-frame!'

When the man did so, the New Hand took the saw and cut him in two. Then he took the halves of the man and threw them into the stream, and the two pieces joined together. The man came down from the stream alive and well, young and frisky. He started to thank the New Hand, but he told him to say nothing at all.

When the New Hand called them back, Sam and his father came running and they were astonished when they saw this young-looking black in place of the old, limping man. They asked all kinds of questions, but the New Hand would not say anything about it, so they gave up, and things went on the same as usual for a time.

Then the old man got word that his mother was very ill, and that he had better go away to visit her. Before he left, he told Sam not to make any trouble for the New Hand; and, if he did, he would get a beating when his father returned. But Sam forgot this just as soon as the old man had gone, and behaved in a very overbearing way towards the help.

Finally, the New Hand said to Sam:

'If you don't stop behaving like this, I'll quit as soon as my time's up, and that's tomorrow.'

But Sam was really insolent, and he said, 'Go now, you fool!'

Well, the next day, sure enough, the New Hand was gone, though nobody saw him go, and nobody passed him on the road or in the woods.

And the very next day, along came the black man who had been made young again, and he brought with him his wife: an old woman, carrying a lovely fat possum and a basket of potatoes which fairly made Sam's mouth water. After passing the time of day, the visitor asked after the New Hand, saying that he wanted him to make the old woman well, as he had done for him.

Sam said, 'Oh, he'll be here tomorrow. Just leave the possum and come again. I'll give it to him when he gets back.'

But the man was too smart for that, and would not leave the things. Sam was afraid that he would lose the possum, so he said:

'The New Hand has gone off to see his sick father, and he told me before he went to carry on and do the same that he did for you.'

So the man told Sam what was wanted, and Sam told the man to go into the woods and shut his eyes. Then Sam sawed the woman in two and threw the pieces into the stream: but there they stayed.

Sam, of course, got very scared, and went down to the water and tried to join the two pieces, but they stayed as they were.

Then the old woman's husband came running and shouting out of the woods, sure that something was wrong. The neighbours collected, and they took Sam away, and he was found guilty of murder.

The judge put on the black cap, and said:

'Hang Sam by the neck until he is dead, and the Lord have mercy on poor Sam.'

Now Sam's old father came running, and he rolled in the dust and begged for Sam's life, but the judge would not let him free. Then everyone went towards the gallows, very solemnly. The judge asked Sam if he had anything to say; and Sam suddenly saw the New Hand, standing in the crowd, and laughing; and Sam thought how badly he had treated that poor man.

So Sam said:

'Brothers and sisters, listen to what I am going to say. Never act haughtily to anyone: because if I hadn't acted in that way to a man who is here in this crowd today, I'd have been heaving saw-logs instead of going to be hanged this day.'

Then all his friends started to cry and roll about, but the New Hand jumped up alongside Sam and said to him:

'Are you sorry for your actions?'

Sam said:

'Indeed I am, and I ask pardon and hope you'll forgive me when I'm gone.'

The New Hand spoke out in a loud voice to the crowd, saying:

'How can you hang this man, when the old woman he is supposed to have killed is standing right over there?'

Sure enough, there she was, standing beside her husband. So they let Sam down, and there were great celebrations. But they have never seen the New Hand, from that day to this, anywhere at all.

The Mastermaid

This story, from the Norse, is translated by Sir George Webbe Dasent, Assistant Editor of the London Times *and Professor of Literature at King's College – from the important collection,* Norse Folktales, *by P. C. Asbjornsen and S. I. Moe, which contains a wide variety of tales from Scandinavia that are also found throughout the world.*

In addition to its remarkable entertainment value, 'The Mastermaid' has for over a century fascinated scholars, some of whom have found it to resemble the classical myth of Jason and Medea very closely. Others have seen in Shakespeare's The Tempest *a reflection of its main theme. The narrative is known from Scotland to the South Seas, in Madagascar and the Buddhist world, in India and – as 'Lady Feather Flight' – in American English tradition. Countless other literary and folktales contain sections or incidents which are to be found in masterly narration in this recension.*

The Aryan and mythological basis of tales was dispersed as a belief by H. Gaidoz (1842–1932). He did this by 'proving' (employing the Muller arguments) that the respected Professor Max Muller was himself only an astronomical myth. For good measure, Gaidoz, editor of the journal Mélusine, *also 'showed' that both Muller's German home and Oxford itself were imaginary places.*

No part of this history of scholarly opinion, fortunately, stands in the way of our enjoyment of this tale.

Once upon a time there was a King who had several sons. The youngest had no rest at home, for nothing else would please him but to go out into the world and try his luck, and after a long time the King was forced to give him leave to go. Now, after he had travelled some days, he came one night to a Giant's house, and there he got a place in the Giant's service. In the morning the Giant went off to herd his goats, and as he left the yard he told the Prince to clean out the stable; 'And after you have done that, you needn't do anything else today; for you must know it is an easy master to whom you have come. But what is set you to do, you must do well, and you mustn't think of going into any of the rooms which are beyond that in which you slept, for if you do I'll take your life.'

'Sure enough, it is an easy master I have got,' said the Prince to himself, as he walked up and down the room, and carolled and sang, for he thought there was plenty of time to clean out the stable.

'But still it would be good fun just to peep into his other rooms, for there must be something in them which he is afraid I should see, since he won't give me leave to go in.'

So he went into the first room, and there was a pot boiling on a hook by the wall, but the Prince saw no fire underneath it. 'I wonder what is inside it,' he thought; and then he dipped a lock of his hair into it, and the hair seemed as if it were turned to copper.

'What a dainty broth,' he said; and he went into the next room. There, too, was a pot hanging by a hook, which bubbled and boiled; but there was no fire under that either.

'I may as well try that too,' said the Prince, as he put another lock of hair in the pot, and it came out all silvered.

'They haven't such rich broth in my father's house,' said the Prince; 'but it all depends on how it tastes,' and with that he went into the third room. There, too, hung a pot and it boiled just as he had seen in the other two rooms. The Prince had a mind to try this too, so he dipped a lock of hair into it, and it came out gilded so that the light gleamed from it.

'Better and better,' said the Prince, 'but if he boils gold here, I wonder what he boils in yonder.'

He thought he might as well see; so he went through the door into the fourth room. Well, there was no pot in there, but there was a Princess, seated on a bench, so lovely that the Prince had never seen anything like her in his born days.

'Oh, in Heaven's name,' she said, 'what do you want here?'

'I got a place here yesterday,' said the Prince.

'A place indeed! Heaven help you out of it.'

'Well, after all, I think I've got an easy master; he hasn't set me much to do today, for after I have cleaned out the stable my day's work is over.'

'Yes, but how will you do it?' she said, 'for if you set to work to clean it, ten pitchforks full will come in for every one you toss out. But I will teach you how to set to work; you must turn the fork upside down, and toss with the handle, and then all the dung will fly out of itself.'

'Yes, I will be sure to do that,' said the Prince; and so he sat there the whole day, for he and the Princess were soon great friends, and had made up their minds to help one another, and so the first day of his service with the Giant was not long. But when the evening drew on she said it would be as well if he got the stable cleaned out before the Giant came home. When he went to the stable he thought he would just see if what she had said were true, and so he began to work like the grooms in his father's stable. But he soon had enough of that, for he hadn't worked a minute before the stable was so full of dung that he hadn't room to stand. Then he did as the Princess bade him, and turned up the fork and worked with the handle, and in a trice the stable was as clean as if it had been scoured. When he had done his work he went back to the room where the Giant had given him leave to be, and began to walk up and down and to carol and sing. So after a bit, home came the Giant with the goats.

'Have you cleaned the stable?' asked the Giant.

'Yes, now it's all right, master,' answered the Prince.

'I'll soon see if it is,' growled the Giant, and strode off to the stable, where he found it just as the Prince had said.

'You've been talking to my Mastermaid, I can see,' said the Giant; 'for you've not got this knowledge out of your own mind!'

'Mastermaid!' said the Prince, who looked as stupid as an owl, 'what sort of thing is that, master? I'd be very glad to see it.'

'Well, well!' said the Giant; 'you'll see her soon enough.'

Next day the Giant set off with his goats again, and before he went he told the Prince to fetch home his horse, which was out at grass on the hillside, and when he had done that he might rest all the day.

'For you must know it is an easy master you have come to,' said the Giant; 'but if you go into any of the rooms I spoke of yesterday, I'll wring your head off.'

So off he went with his flock of goats.

'An easy master you are indeed,' said the Prince; 'but for all that, I'll just go and have a chat with your Mastermaid; maybe she'll soon be mine instead of yours.' So he went in to her, and she asked him what he had to do that day.

'Oh, nothing to be afraid of,' said he; 'I've only to go up the hillside to fetch his horse.'

'Very well, and how will you set about it?' said she.

'Well, for that matter, there's no great art in riding

a horse home. I've ridden fresher horses before,' said the Prince.

'Ah, but this isn't so easy a task as you think,' said she, 'but I'll teach you how to do it. When you get near it, fire and flame will come out of its nostrils, but look out, and take the bit which hangs behind the door yonder, and throw it right into its jaws and it will grow so tame that you may do what you like.'

The Prince said he would do that; and so he sat in there the whole day, talking and chattering with the Mastermaid about one thing and another; but they always came back to how happy they would be if only they could only be with one another and get well away from the Giant. The Prince would have forgotten both the horse and the hillside, if the Mastermaid hadn't put him in mind of them when evening drew on, telling him he had better set out to fetch the horse before the Giant came home. So he set off, and took the bit which hung in the corner, ran up the hill, and it wasn't long before he met the horse, with fire and flame streaming out of its nostrils. But he watched his time, and as the horse came open-jawed up to him, he threw the bit into its mouth and it stood, quiet as a lamb. After that it was no great matter to ride it home and put it up. Then the Prince went into his room again, and began to carol and sing.

So the Giant came home again at evening with his goats; and the first words he said were:

'Have you brought my horse down from the hill?'

'Yes master, that I have,' said the Prince, 'and a better horse I never bestrode; I rode him straight home, and put him up safe and sound.'

'I'll soon see to that,' said the Giant, and he ran out to the stable, and there stood the horse just as the Prince had said.

'You've talked to my Mastermaid, I'll be bound, for you haven't got this out of your own mind,' said the Giant again.

'Yesterday master talked of this Mastermaid, and today it's the same story,' said the Prince, who pretended to be silly and stupid. 'Why don't you show me the thing at once? I should like to see it only once in my life.'

'Oh, if that's all,' said the Giant, 'you'll see her soon enough.'

The third day at dawn the Giant went off to the wood again with his goats; but before he went he said to the Prince:

'Today you must go to Hell and fetch my fire-tax. When you have done that you can rest yourself all day, for you must know it is an easy master you have come to,' and with that off he went.

'Easy master, indeed!' said the Prince. 'You may be easy, but you set me hard tasks all the same. But I may as well see if I can find your Mastermaid, as you call her. I daresay she'll tell me what to do,' and so in he went to her again.

So when the Mastermaid asked what the Giant had set him to do that day, he told her how he was to go to Hell and fetch the fire-tax.

'And how will you set about it?' asked the Mastermaid.

'Oh, that you must tell me,' said the Prince. 'I have never been to Hell in my life; and even if I knew the way, I don't know how much I am to ask for.'

'Well, I'll soon tell you,' said the Mastermaid; 'you must go to the steep rock away yonder, under the hillside, and take the club that lies there, and knock on the face of the rock. Then there will come out one all glistening with fire; to him you must tell your errand; and when he asks you how much you will have, mind you say, "As much as I can carry".'

The Prince sat in there with the Mastermaid all that day too; and though evening drew on, he would have sat there till now, had not the Mastermaid told him that it was high time to be off to Hell to fetch the Giant's fire-tax before he came home. So he went on his way, and did just as the Mastermaid had told him; and when he reached the rock he took up the club and gave a great thump. Then the rock opened, and out came one whose face glistened, and out of whose eyes and nostrils flew sparks of fire.

'What is your will?' said he.

'I have come from the Giant to fetch his fire-tax,'

said the Prince.

'How much will you have then?' said the other.

'No more than I am able to carry,' said the Prince.

'Lucky for you that you did not ask for a whole horse-load,' said he who came out of the rock; 'but come now into the rock with me, and you shall have it.'

So the Prince went in with him, and you may fancy what heaps and heaps of gold and silver he saw lying in there just like stones in a gravel-pit. He got a load just as big as he was able to carry, and set off home with it. Now, when the Giant came home with his goats at even, the Prince went into his room and began to carol and sing as he had done the evenings before.

'Have you been to Hell after my fire-tax?' roared the Giant.

'I have master,' answered the Prince.

'Where have you put it?' said the Giant.

'There stands the sack on the bench,' said the Prince.

'I'll soon see to that,' said the Giant, who strode off to the bench, and there he saw the sack so full that the gold and silver dropped out on the floor as soon as he untied the string.

'You've been talking to my Mastermaid, that I can see,' said the Giant. 'But if you have, I'll wring your head off.'

'Mastermaid!' said the Prince; 'yesterday you talked of this Mastermaid, and today you talk of her again, and the day before yesterday it was the same story. I only wish I could see what sort of thing she is!'

'Well, well, wait till tomorrow,' said the Giant, 'and then I'll take you to her myself.'

'Thank you kindly, master,' said the Prince. 'But it's only a joke, I'll be bound.'

So next day the Giant took him to the Mastermaid, and said to her:

'Now you must cut his throat, and boil him in the great big pot, and when broth is ready just give me a call.'

After that he lay down on the bench to sleep, and began to snore so, that it sounded like thunder over hills.

So the Mastermaid took a knife, and cut the Prince in his little finger, and let three drops of blood fall on a three-legged stool; and after that she took old rags and soles of shoes, and all the rubbish she could lay hands on, and put them into the pot. Then she filled a chest full of ground gold, and took a lump of salt, a flask of water that hung behind the door, and she took, besides, a golden apple, and two golden chickens, and off she set with the Prince from the Giant's house as fast as they could. When they had gone a little way they came to the sea, and after that they sailed in a ship over the sea.

When the Giant had slumbered a good bit, he began to stretch himself as he lay on the bench, and called out, 'Isn't it done yet?'

'Done to a turn,' said the third drop of blood.

Then the Giant rose up, and began to rub his eyes, but he couldn't see who it was that was talking to him, so he searched and called for the Mastermaid, but no-one answered.

'Ah well! I dare say she's just run out of doors for a bit,' he thought, and took up a spoon and went up to the pot to taste the broth; but he found nothing but shoe-soles and rags and such stuff; and it was all boiled up together, so that he couldn't tell which was thick and which was thin. As soon as he saw this, he could tell how things had gone, and he got so angry he scarce knew which leg to stand upon. Away he went after the Prince and the Mastermaid, till the wind whistled behind him; but before long he came to the water and couldn't cross it.

'Never mind,' he said, 'I know a cure for this. I've only got to call on my stream-sucker.'

So he called on his stream-sucker, and he came and stooped down, and took one, two, three, gulps; and then the water fell so much in the sea that the Giant could see the Mastermaid and the Prince sailing in their ship.

'Now you must cast out the lump of salt,' said the Mastermaid.

So the Prince threw it overboard, and it grew up into a mountain so high, right across the sea, that the Giant couldn't pass it, and the stream-sucker couldn't help him by swilling any more water.

'Never mind,' cried the Giant; 'there's a cure for this too.' So he called on his hill-borer to come and bore through the mountain, that the stream-sucker might creep through and take another swill; but just as they had made a hole through the hill, and the stream-sucker was about to drink, the Mastermaid told the Prince to throw overboard a drop or two out of the flask. Then the sea was just as full as ever, and before the stream-sucker could take another gulp, they reached the land and were saved from the Giant.

They made up their minds to go home to the Prince's father, but the Prince would not hear of the Mastermaid's walking, for he thought it seemly neither for her nor for him.

'Just wait here ten minutes,' he said, 'while I go home after the seven horses which stand in my father's stall. It is not far and I shan't be long, but I will not hear of my sweetheart walking to my father's palace.'

'Ah!' said the Mastermaid, 'don't leave me, for if you once get home to the palace you'll forget me, I know you will.'

'Oh!' said he, 'how can I forget you; you with whom I have gone through so much, and whom I love so dearly?'

There was no help for it, he went home to fetch the coach and seven horses, and she was to wait for him by the seaside. So at last the Mastermaid was forced to let him have his way; she only said:

'Now, when you get home, don't stop so much as to say good day to anyone. Go straight to the stable and put up the horses, and drive back as quick as you can; for they will all come about you, but act as though you did not see them. Above all things, mind you do not taste a morsel of food, for if you do, we shall both come to grief.'

All this the Prince promised; but he thought all the way that there was little fear of his forgetting her.

Now, just as he came home to the palace, one of his brothers was thinking of holding his bridal feast, and the bride and all her kith and kin had just come to the palace. So they all thronged round him, and asked about this thing and that, and wanted him to go in with them; but he made as though he did not see them, and went straight to the stall and got out the horses. And when they saw they could not get him to go in, they came out to him with meat and drink, and the best of everything they had got ready for the feast; but the Prince would not taste so much as a crumb, and got the horses ready as fast as he could. At last the bride's sister rolled an apple across the yard to him, saying:

'Well, if you won't eat anything else, you may as well take a bite of this, for you must be both hungry and thirsty after so long a journey.'

So he took up an apple and bit a piece out of

it; but he had scarce done so before he forgot the Mastermaid, and how he was to drive back for her.

'Well, I think I must be mad,' he said; 'what am I to do with this coach and horses?'

So he put the horses up again, and went along with the others into the palace and it was soon settled that he should have as his wife the bride's sister, who had rolled the apple over to him.

There sat the Mastermaid by the seashore, and waited and waited for the Prince, but no Prince came; so at last she went up from the shore, and after she had gone a bit she came to a little hut, which lay by itself in a copse close by the King's palace. She went in and asked if she might lodge there. An old dame owned the hut, and a cross-grained scolding hag she was as ever you saw. At first she would not hear of the Mastermaid lodging in her house, but at last, for fair words and high rent, the Mastermaid got leave to be there. Now the hut was as dark and dirty as a pigsty, so the Mastermaid said she would clear it up a little, so that their house might look like other people's. The old hag did not like this either, and showed her teeth and was cross; but the Mastermaid did not mind her. She took her chest of gold, and threw a handful or so into the fire, and the gold melted, and bubbled and boiled over out of the grate, and spread itself over the whole hut till it was gilded both outside and in. But as soon as the gold began to bubble and boil, the old hag got so afraid that she tried to run out as if the Evil One were at her heels; and as she ran out of the door, she forgot to stoop, and gave her head such a knock against the lintel that she broke her neck, and that was the end of her.

Next morning the Constable passed that way, and he could scarce believe his eyes when he saw the golden hut shining and glistening away in the copse; but he was still more astonished when he went in and saw the lovely maiden who sat there. To make a long story short, he fell over head and ears in love with her, and begged and prayed her to become his wife.

'Well, but have you much money?' asked the Mastermaid. He said he was not so badly off, and off he went home to fetch the money, and when he came back he brought a half-bushel sack, and set it down on the bench. So the Mastermaid said she would have him, since he was so rich; but they were scarce in bed before she said she must get up again:

'For I have forgotten to make up the fire.'

'Don't stir out of bed,' said the Constable; 'I'll see to it.'

So he jumped out of bed, and stood on the hearth.

'As soon as you have got hold of the shovel, just tell me,' said the Mastermaid.

'Well, I am holding it now,' said the Constable.

Then the Mastermaid said:

'God grant that you may hold the shovel, and the

shovel you, and may you heap hot burning coals over yourself till morning breaks.'

So there stood the Constable all night long, shovelling hot burning coals over himself; and though he begged, and prayed, and wept, the coals were not a bit colder for that; but as soon as day broke, and he had power to cast away the shovel, he did not stay long, but set off as if the Evil One or the bailiff were at his heels. All who met him stared their eyes out at him, for he cut capers as though he were mad, and he could not have looked in worse plight if he had been flayed and tanned, and everyone wondered what had befallen him, but he told no one where he had been, for shame's sake.

Next day the Attorney passed by the place where the Mastermaid lived, and he, too, saw how it shone and glistened in the copse. He turned aside to find out who owned the hut; and when he came in and saw the lovely maiden he fell more in love with her than the Constable, and began to woo her in hot haste.

Well, the Mastermaid asked him, as she had asked the Constable, if he had a good lot of money, and the Attorney said he wasn't so badly off; and as proof he went home to fetch his money. So he came back with a great fat sack of money – a whole bushel sack – and set it down on the bench; and the long and the short of the matter was, that he was to have her, and they went to bed. But all at once the Mastermaid had forgotten to shut the door of the porch, and she must get up and make it fast for the night.

'What, you do that!' said the Attorney, 'while I lie here; that can never be; lie still while I go and do it.'

So up he jumped like a pea on a drum-head, and ran out into the porch.

'Tell me,' said the Mastermaid, 'when you have hold of the door-latch.'

'I've got hold of it now,' said the Attorney.

'God grant then,' said the Mastermaid, 'that you may hold the door, and the door you, and that you may go from wall to wall till day dawns.'

What a dance the Attorney had all night long; such a waltz he never had before, and I don't think he would much care if he never had such a waltz again. Now he pulled the door forward, and then the door pulled him back, and so he went on, now dashed into one corner of the porch, and now into the other, till he was almost battered to death. At first he began to curse and swear, and then to beg and pray, but the door cared for nothing but holding its own till break of day. As soon as it let go its hold, off set the Attorney, leaving behind him his money to pay for his night's lodgings, and forgetting his courtship altogether, for, to tell the truth, he was afraid lest the house-door should come dancing after him. All who met him stared and gaped at him, for he too cut capers like a madman, and he could not have looked in worse plight if he had spent the whole night in butting against a flock of rams.

The third day the Sheriff passed that way, and he also saw the golden hut, and turned aside to find out who lived there; and he had scarce set eyes on the Mastermaid before he began to woo her. So she answered him as she had answered the other two. If he had lots of money she would have him; if not, he might go about his business. Well, the Sheriff said he wasn't badly off, and he would go home and fetch the money; and when he came again he had a bigger sack even than the Attorney – it must have been at least a bushel and a half, and put it down on the bench. So it was soon settled that he was to have the Mastermaid, but they had scarce gone to bed before the Mastermaid said she had forgotten to bring home the calf from the meadow, so she must get up and drive him into the stall. Then the Sheriff swore by all the powers that should never be, and, stout and fat as he was, up he jumped as nimbly as a kitten.

'Well, only tell me when you've got hold of the calf's tail,' said the Mastermaid.

'Now I have hold of it,' said the Sheriff.

'God grant,' said the Mastermaid, 'that you may hold the calf's tail, and the calf's tail you, and that you may make a tour of the world together till day dawns.'

Well, you may just fancy how the Sheriff had to stretch his legs; away they went, the calf and he, over high and low, across hill and dale, and the more the Sheriff cursed and swore, the faster the calf ran and jumped. At dawn of day the poor Sheriff was well nigh broken-winded, and so glad was he to let go of the calf's tail that he forgot his sack of money and everything else. As he was a fat man, he went a little slower than the Attorney and the Constable, but the slower he went the more time people had to gape and stare at him; and I must say they made good use of their time, for he was terribly tattered and torn, after his dance with the calf.

Next day was fixed for the wedding at the palace, and the eldest brother was to drive to church with his bride, and the younger, who had lived with the Giant, with the bride's sister. But when they had got into the coach, and were just going to drive off, one of the trace-pins snapped off; and though they made at least three in its place, they all broke, from whatever sort of wood they were made. So time went on and on, and they couldn't get to church, and everyone grew very downcast. But all at once the Constable said, for he too was bidden to the wedding, that yonder, away in the copse, lived a maiden:

'And if you can only get her to lend you the handle of her shovel with which she makes up her fire, I know very well it will hold,' he said.

They sent a messenger on the spot, with a message to the maiden to know if they couldn't get the loan of her shovel of which the Constable had spoken, and the maiden said 'yes' they might have it; so they got a trace-pin which wasn't likely to snap.

But all at once, just as they were driving off, the bottom of the coach tumbled to bits. So they went to work to make a new bottom as they best might; but it mattered not how many nails they put into it, nor of what wood they made it, as soon as ever they got the bottom well into the coach and were driving off, snap it went in two again, and they were even worse off than when they lost the trace-pin. Just then the Attorney said – for if the Constable was there, you may be sure the Attorney was there too – 'Away yonder, in the copse, lives a maiden, and if you could only get her to lend you one-half of her porch-door, I know it can hold together.'

They sent another message to the maiden, and asked so prettily if they couldn't have the loan of the gilded porch-door which the Attorney had talked of; and they got it on the spot. So they were just setting out; but now the horses were not strong enough to draw the coach, though there were six of them, then they put on eight, and ten, and twelve, but the more they put on, and the more the coachman whipped, the more the coach wouldn't stir an inch. By this time it was far on in the day, and everyone about the palace was in the dumps; for to church they must go, and yet it looked as if they should never get there. So at last the Sheriff said that yonder, in the gilded hut in the copse, lived a maiden, and if they could only get the loan of her calf…

'I know it can drag the coach, though it were as heavy as a mountain,' he said.

They all thought it would look silly to be drawn to church by a calf, but there was no help for it, so they had to send a third time, and asked in the King's name it they couldn't get the loan of the calf the Sheriff had spoken of, and the Mastermaid let them have it on the spot, for she was not going to say 'no' this time either. So they put the calf on before the horses, and waited to see if it would do any good, and away went the coach over high and low, and stock and stone, so that they could scarce draw their breath. Sometimes they were on the ground and sometimes up in the air, and when they reached the church, the calf began to run round and round it like a spinning jenny, so that they had hard work to get out of the coach, and into the church. When they went back, it was the same story, only they went faster, and they reached the palace almost before they knew they had set out.

Now when they sat down to dinner, the Prince who had served with the Giant said he thought they ought to ask the maiden who had lent them her shovel-handle and porch-door and calf, to come up to the palace.

'For,' said he, 'if we hadn't got these three things,

we should have been sticking here still.'

The King thought that only fair, so he sent five of his best men down to the gilded hut to greet the maiden from the King, and to ask her if she would be so good as to come up and dine at the palace.

'Greet the King from me,' said the Mastermaid, 'and tell him, if he's too good to come to me, so am I too good to go to him.'

So the King had to go himself, and then the Mastermaid went up with him without more ado; and as the King thought she was more than she seemed to be, he sat her down in the highest seat by the side of the youngest bridegroom.

Now, when they had sat a little while at table, the Mastermaid took out her golden apple, and the golden cock and hen, which she had carried off from the Giant, and put them down on the table before her, and the cock and hen began at once to peck at one another, and to fight for the golden apple.

'Look,' said the Prince; 'see how those two strive for the apple.'

'Yes!' said the Mastermaid; 'so we two strove to get away that time when we were together on the hillside.'

Then the spell was broken, and the Prince knew her again, and how glad he was. But as for the witch who had rolled the apple over to him, he had her torn to pieces between twenty-four horses, so that there was not a bit of her left. After that they held the wedding in real earnest; and though they were still stiff and footsore, the Constable, the Attorney and the Sheriff kept it up with the best of them.

The Hermit

'The Hermit' is one of the favourite tales of the Sufi teachers of the East, illustrating the lack of insight of the ordinary individual. A version of it by the poet Thomas Parnell was published in 1721, and the legend was regarded as his invention until 1773; though it was later thought to have come from Spain and to be an Arabian composition. It had, however, already been printed in the English translation of the medieval monkish tales, the Gesta Romanorum, *in 1703, and it was thought to be Voltairean, through that philosopher's use of it in* Zadig, *in 1748. It has been found as a popular tale in Sicily and Spain – both formerly Islamic territories – and its first appearance in literature was in the* Koran, *nearly fourteen hundred years ago. In Chapter 18 of the Muslim holy book, the account is attributed to Moses' instruction by an unknown mysterious figure, generally believed to be the apparition Khidr, later regarded as the guide of the Sufi mystics. This is Voltaire's presentation.*

In the reign of King Moabdar there lived at Babylon a young man named Zadig. He was handsome, rich, and naturally good-hearted; and at the moment when this story opens, he was travelling on foot to see the world, and to learn philosophy and wisdom. But, hitherto, he had encountered so much misery, and endured so many terrible disasters, that he had become tempted to rebel against the will of Heaven, and to believe that the Providence which rules the world neglects the good, and lets the evil prosper. In this unhappy spirit he was one day walking on the banks of the Euphrates, when he chanced to meet a venerable hermit, whose snowy beard descended to his girdle, and who carried in his hand a scroll which he was reading with attention. Zadig stopped, and made him a low bow. The hermit returned the salutation with an air so kindly, and so noble, that Zadig felt a curiosity to speak to him. He enquired what scroll was that which he was reading.

'It is the Book of Destiny,' replied the hermit, 'would you like to read it?'

He handed it to Zadig; but the latter, though he knew a dozen languages, could not understand a word of it. His curiosity increased.

'You appear to be in trouble,' said the kindly hermit.

'Alas!' said Zadig, 'I have cause to be so.'

'If you will allow me,' said the hermit, 'I will accompany you. Perhaps I may be useful to you. I am sometimes able to console the sorrowful.'

Zadig felt a deep respect for the appearance, the white beard, and the mysterious scroll of the old hermit, and perceived that his conversation was that of a superior mind. The old man spoke of destiny, of justice, of morality, of the chief good of life, of human frailty, of virtue and of vice, with so much power and eloquence that Zadig felt himself attracted by a kind of charm, and besought the hermit not to leave him until they should return to Babylon.

'I ask you the same favour,' said the hermit. 'Promise me that, whatever I may do, you will keep me company for several days.'

Zadig gave the promise; and they set forth together.

That night the travellers arrived at a grand mansion. The hermit begged for food and lodging for himself and his companion. The porter, who might have been mistaken for a prince, ushered them in with a contemptuous air of welcome. The chief servant showed them the magnificent apartments; and they were then admitted to the bottom of the table, where the master of the mansion did not condescend to cast a glance at them. They were, however, served with delicacies in profusion, and after dinner washed their hands in a golden basin set with emeralds and rubies. They were then conducted for the night into a beautiful apartment; and the next morning, before they left the castle, a servant brought them each a piece of gold.

'The master of the house,' said Zadig, as they went their way, 'appears to be a generous man, although a trifle haughty. He practises a noble hospitality.' As he spoke, he perceived that a kind of large pouch which the hermit carried appeared singularly distended; within it was the golden basin, set with precious stones, which the old man had purloined. Zadig was amazed; but he said nothing.

At noon the hermit stopped before a little house, in which lived a wealthy miser, and once more asked for hospitality. An old valet in a shabby coat received them very rudely, showed them into the stable, and set before them a few rotten olives, some mouldy bread, and beer which had turned sour. The hermit ate and drank with as much content as he had shown the night before; then, addressing the old valet, who had kept his eye upon them to make sure that they stole nothing, he gave him the two gold pieces which they had received that morning, and thanked him for his kind attention. 'Be so good,' he added, 'as to let me see your master.'

The astonished valet showed them in.

'Most mighty signor,' said the hermit, 'I can only render you my humble thanks for the noble manner in which you have received us. I beseech you to accept this golden basin as a token of my gratitude.'

The miser almost fell backwards with amazement. The hermit, without waiting for him to recover, set off with speed, with his companion.

'Holy Father,' said Zadig, 'what does all this mean? You seem to me to resemble other men in nothing. You steal a golden basin set with jewels from a signor who receives you with magnificence, and you give it to a curmudgeon who treats you with indignity.'

'My son,' replied the hermit, 'this mighty lord, who only welcomes travellers through vanity and to display his riches, will henceforth grow wiser, while the miser will be taught to practise hospitality. Be amazed at nothing, and follow me.'

Zadig knew not whether he was dealing with the most foolish or the wisest of all men. But the hermit spoke with such ascendancy that Zadig, who besides was fettered by his promise, had no choice except to follow him.

That night they came to an agreeable house, of simple aspect, and showing signs of neither prodigality nor avarice. The owner was a philosopher, who had left the world, and who studied peacefully the rules of virtue and of wisdom, and who yet was happy and contented. He had built this calm retreat to please himself, and he received the strangers in it with a frankness which displayed no sign of ostentation. He conducted them himself to a comfortable chamber, where he made them rest awhile; then he returned to lead them to a dainty little supper. During their conversation they agreed that the affairs of this world are not always regulated by the opinions of the wisest men. But the hermit still maintained that the ways of Providence are wrapped in mystery, and that men do wrong to pass their judgement on a universe of which they only see the smallest part. Zadig wondered how a person who committed such mad acts could reason so correctly.

At length, after a conversation as agreeable as instructive, the host conducted the two travellers to their apartment, and thanked heaven for sending him two visitors so wise and virtuous. He offered them some money, but so frankly that they could not feel offended. The old man declined, and desired to say farewell, as he intended to depart for Babylon at break of day. They therefore parted on the warmest terms, and Zadig, above all, was filled with kindly feelings towards so amiable a man.

When the hermit and himself were in their chamber, they spent some time in praises of their host. At break of day the old man woke his comrade.

'We must be going,' he remarked. 'But while everyone is still asleep, I wish to leave this worthy man a pledge of my esteem.' With these words, he took a torch and set the house on fire.

Zadig burst forth into cries of horror, and would have stopped the frightful act. But the hermit, by superior strength, drew him away. The house was in a blaze; and the old man, who was now a good way off with his companion, looked back calmly at the burning pile.

'Heaven be praised!' he cried. 'Our kind host's house is destroyed from top to bottom!'

At these words Zadig knew not whether he should burst out laughing, call the reverend father an old rascal, knock him down, or run away. But he did none of these things. Still subdued by the superior manner of the hermit, he followed him against his will to their next lodging.

This was the dwelling of a good and charitable widow, who had a nephew of fourteen, her only hope and joy. She did her best to use the travellers well; and the next morning she bade her nephew guide them safely past a certain bridge, which, having recently been broken, had become dangerous to cross over. The youth, eager to oblige them, led the way.

'Come,' said the hermit, when they were half across the bridge, 'I must show my gratitude towards your aunt,' and as he spoke he seized the young man by the hair and threw him into the river. The youth fell, reappeared for an instant on the surface, and then was swallowed by the torrent.

'Oh, monster!' exclaimed Zadig, 'oh, most detestable of men!'

'You promised me more patience,' interrupted the old man. 'Listen! Beneath the ruins of that house which Providence saw fit to set on fire, the owner will discover an enormous treasure; while this young man, whose existence Providence cut short, would have killed his aunt within a year, and you yourself in two.'

'Who told you so, barbarian?' cried Zadig. 'And even if you read the issue in your Book of Destiny, who gave you power to drown a youth who never injured you?'

While he spoke, he saw that the old man had a beard no longer, and that his face had become fair and young; his hermit's dress had disappeared: four white wings covered his majestic form, and shone with dazzling lustre.

'Angel of heaven!' cried Zadig, 'you are then descended from the skies to teach an erring mortal to submit to the eternal laws?'

'Men,' replied the angel Jezrael, 'judge all things without knowledge; and you, of all men, most deserved to be enlightened. The world imagines that the youth who has just perished fell by chance into the water, and that by a like chance the rich man's house was set on fire. But there is no such thing as chance; all is trial, or punishment, or foresight. Feeble mortal, cease to argue and rebel against what you ought to adore!'

As he spoke these words the angel took his flight to heaven. And Zadig fell upon his knees.

The Maiden Wiser than the Tsar

Such a profusion of the traditional stories of the world are to be found in the Balkans that it has even been suggested that this area is one of the original homes of the folktale. Hardly a genre – Slavic, Greek, Turkic, Latin, Arabian or Jewish – is unrepresented. Through the Western European connection, the tales most often found in Germany, France, Italy are abundant; from the north are recognisable variants of the lore of the Russian and Scandinavian, as well as Mongolian traditions; and recitals from the ancient classical books are still very much in evidence.

This Serbian story follows the very ancient pattern which has been called 'The Clever Girl', and in contemporary terms it may be regarded as an example of the feminine use of non-linear thinking on which contemporary problem-solving ideas are increasingly based. The tale is sometimes prefaced by the account of the girl carving a cooked fowl at a dinner where the Prince is present. Nobody can understand why she apportions the pieces in the way in which she does; instead of giving portions to the diners in accordance with their rank, she assigns them symbolically. The Prince overhears her explaining 'The head to the head of the family, the wings for me to fly to catch a husband', and falls in love with her. This completes the symbolism of the filling of a need, where the Prince represents linear thinking and needs the other form of wisdom represented by the girl. As an illustration of the respective functions of the two brain hemispheres, recently recorded by scientists, one could hardly expect a better example than this most ancient tale of Serbia.

Once upon a time there was a poor man who had one daughter.

Now, this girl was amazingly wise, seemed to have knowledge far beyond her years, and often said things which surprised her own father.

One day, being without a penny, the poor man went to the Tsar to beg.

The Tsar, astonished at the man's cultivated way of saying things, asked him where he had learned such phrases.

'From my daughter,' he replied.

'But where was your daughter taught?' asked the Tsar.

'God and our poverty have made her wise,' was the answer.

'Here is some money for your immediate needs,' said the Tsar, 'and here are thirty eggs; command your daughter in my name to hatch them for me. If she does this successfully, you shall both have rich presents, but if she does not, you will be put to the torture.'

The man went home and took the eggs to his daughter. She examined them, and weighed one or two in her hands. Then she realised that they were hard-boiled. So she said, 'Father, wait until tomorrow, maybe I can think what can be done about this.'

Next day, she was up early, having thought of a solution, and boiled some beans. She gave her father a small bag of the beans, and said:

'Go with the plough and oxen, father, and start ploughing beside the road where the Tsar will pass on his way to church. When he puts his head out of the carriage window, call out "Go on, good oxen, plough the land so that these boiled beans will grow well!"'

The father did as she told him, and sure enough, the Tsar put his head out of the window of his carriage to watch the man at work, and, hearing what was being shouted, said, 'Stupid fellow, how can you expect boiled beans to produce anything?'

Primed by his daughter, the simple man called out, 'Just as from boiled eggs chickens can be produced!'

So, laughing, the Tsar went on his way, knowing that the girl had outwitted him.

But it was not to end there.

The next day the Tsar sent a courtier to the poor man with a bundle of flax, saying, 'This flax must be made into sails for my ship by tomorrow; otherwise, you will be executed.'

Weeping, the man went home, but his daughter said, 'Have no fear, I shall think of something.'

In the morning she came to him and gave him a small block of wood, and said, 'Tell the Tsar that if he can have all the tools necessary for spinning and weaving made out of this piece of wood, I will do the material for his sails out of the bunch of flax.'

He did so, and the Tsar was further impressed by the girl's answer. But he put a small glass into the man's hand and said:

'Go, take this to your daughter, and ask her to empty the sea with this so that I may enlarge my dominions with precious new pastures.'

The man went home, and gave his daughter the glass, telling her that the ruler had demanded yet another impossibility.

'Go to bed.' she said, 'I will think of something by bringing my mind to bear upon it all night.'

In the morning she said, 'Go to the Tsar and tell him that if he can dam up all the rivers of the world with this bundle of tow, then I will empty the sea for him.'

The father went back to the Tsar and told him what his daughter had said. The Tsar, seeing that she was wiser than himself, asked that she be brought to court forthwith. When she appeared he asked her:

'What is it that can be heard at the greatest distance?'

Without any hesitation she replied at once:

'The thunder and the lie can be heard at the greatest distance, O Tsar.'

Astonished, the Tsar grasped his beard, and then, turning to his courtiers asked:

'What is my beard worth, do you think?'

Each of them began to say what they thought the Tsar's beard was worth, making the value higher and higher, hoping to curry favour with His Majesty. Then, he said to the maiden:

'And what do you think my beard is worth, my child?'

Everyone looked on in amazement as she replied:

'Your Majesty's beard is worth every bit as much as three summer rains!'

The Tsar, greatly astonished, said:

'You have guessed rightly; I shall marry you and make you my wife this very day.'

So the girl became the Tsarina. But just when the wedding was over, she said to the Tsar:

'I have one request to make; be graciously pleased to write with your own hand that if you, or anyone in your court be displeased with me, and I had to go away, I should be allowed to take with me any one thing which I liked best.'

Enamoured of the beautiful maiden, the Tsar asked for pen and parchment, and at once wrote, sealing the document with his own ruby ring, as she had requested.

The years passed most happily for both of them, then one day the Tsar had a heated argument with the Tsarina and said:

'Go, I desire that you leave this palace, never to return!'

'I shall go tomorrow, then,' said the young Tsarina dutifully. 'Only allow me one more night here to prepare myself for the journey home.'

The Tsar agreed, and she gave him his bedtime

herbal drink with her usual care.

No sooner had the Tsar drunk the potion than he fell asleep. The Tsarina had the Tsar carried to a coach, and they went to her father's cottage.

When the morning came, the Tsar, who had spent a tranquil night, woke, and looked around him in amazement.

'Treason!' he roared. 'Where am I, and whose prisoner?'

'Mine, your majesty,' said the Tsarina sweetly. 'Your parchment, written with your own hand is here,' and she showed him where he had written that if she had to leave the palace she could take with her that which she liked best.

Hearing this, the Tsar laughed heartily, and declared that his affection for her had returned.

'My great love for you, O Tsar,' said she, 'has made me do this bold thing, but I risked death to do it, so you must see that my love is indeed very great.'

Then they were united, and lived happily together for the rest of their lives.

FINIS